# THE

# LAW OF

# SUCCESS

## LESSONS TWELVE AND THIRTEEN

Teaching, for the First Time in the History of the World, the True
Philosophy upon which all Personal Success is Built.

## BY

### NAPOLEON HILL

Originally published by The RALSTON UNIVERSITY PRESS
MERIDEN, CONN.

© Copyright 2006 – BN Publishing

www.bnpublishing.com

Printed in the U.S.A.

# Lesson Twelve

## CONCENTRATION

### "You Can Do It if You Believe You Can!"

THIS lesson occupies a key-stone position in this course, for the reason that the psychological law upon which it is based is of vital importance to every other lesson of the course.

Let us define the word concentration, as it is here used, as follows: "Concentration is the act of focusing the mind upon a given desire until ways and means for its realization have been worked out and successfully put into operation."

Two important laws enter into the act of concentrating the mind on a given desire. One is the law of Auto-suggestion and the other is the law of habit. The former having been fully described in a previous lesson of this course, we will now briefly describe the law of habit.

Habit grows out of environment - out of doing the same thing in the same way over and over again - out of repetition - out of thinking the same thoughts overand over - and, when once formed, it resembles a cement block that has hardened in the mold - in that it is hard to break.

Habit is the basis of all memory training, a fact which you may easily demonstrate in remembering the name of a person whom you have just met, by repeating that name over and over until you have fixed it permanently and plainly in your mind.

"The force of education is so great that we may mold the minds and manners of the young into whatever shape we please and give the impressions of such habits as shall ever afterwards remain." -Atterbury.

Except on rare occasions when the mind rises above environment, the human mind draws the material out of which thought is created, from the surrounding environment, and habit crystallizes this thought into a: permanent fixture and stores it away in the subconscious mind where it becomes a vital part of our personality which silently influences our actions, forms our prejudices and our biases, and controls our opinions.

5

A great philosopher had in mind the power of habit when he said: "We first endure, then pity, and finally embrace," in speaking of the manner in which honest men come to indulge in crime.

Habit may be likened to the grooves on a phonograph record, while the mind may be likened to the needle point that fits into that groove. When any habit has been well formed (by repetition of thought or action) the mind attaches itself to and follows that habit as closely as the phonograph needle follows the groove in the wax record, no matter what may be the nature of that habit.

We begin to see, therefore, the importance of selecting our environment with the greatest of care, because environment is the mental feeding ground out of which the food that goes into our minds is extracted.

Environment very largely supplies the food and materials out of which we create thought, and habit crystallizes these into permanency. You of course understand that "environment" is the sum total of sources through which you are influenced by and through the aid of the five senses of seeing, hearing, smelling, tasting and feeling.

"Habit is force which is generally recognized by the average thinking person, but which is commonly viewed in its adverse aspect to the exclusion of its favorable phase. It has been well said that all men are 'the creatures of habit,' and that 'habit is a cable; we weave a thread of it each day and it becomes so strong that we cannot break it.'

"If it be true that habit becomes a cruel tyrant, ruling and compelling men against their will, desire, and inclination - and this is true in many cases - the question naturally arises in the thinking mind whether this mighty force cannot be harnessed and controlled in the service of men, just as have other forces of Nature. If this result can be accomplished, then man may master habit and set it to work, instead of being a slave to it and serving it faithfully though complinings. And the modern psychologists tell us in no uncertain tones that habit may certainly be thus mastered, harnessed and set to work, instead of being allowed to dominate one's actions and character. And thousands of people have applied this new knowledge and have turned the force of habit into new channels,and have compelled it to work their machinery of action, instead of being allowed to run to waste, or else permitted to sweep away the structures that men have erected with care and expense, or to destroy fertile mental fields.

"A habit is a 'mental path' over which our actions have traveled for some time, each passing making the path a little deeper and a little wider. If you have to walk over a field or through a forest, you know how natural it is for you to choose the clearest path in preference to the less worn ones, and greatly in preference to stepping out across the field or through the woods and making a new path. And the line of mental action is precisely the same. It is movement along the lines of least resistance - passage over the well-worn path. Habits are created by repetition and are formed in accordance to a natural law, observable in all animate things and some would say in inanimate things as well. As an instance of the latter, it is pointed out that a piece of paper once folded in a certain way will fold along the same lines the next time. And all users of sewing machines, or other delicate pieces of machinery, know that as a machine or instrument is once 'broken in' so will it tend to run thereafter. The same law is also observable in the case of musical instruments. Clothing or gloves form into creases according to the person using them, and these creases once formed will always be in effect, notwithstanding repeated pressings. Rivers and streams of water cut their courses through the land, and thereafter flow along the habit-course. The law is in operation everywhere.

"These illustrations will help you to form the ideaof the nature of habit, and will aid you in forming new mental paths - new mental creases. And - remember this always - the best (and one might say the only) way in which old habits may be removed is to form new habits to counteract and replace the undesirable ones. Form new mental paths over which to travel, and the old ones will soon become less distinct and in time will practically fill up from disuse. Every time you travel over the path of the desirable mental habit, you make the path deeper and wider, and make it so much easier to travel it thereafter. This mental path-making is a very important thing, and I cannot urge upon you too strongly the injunction to start to work making the desirable mental paths over which you wish to travel. Practice, practice, practice - be a good path-maker."

The following are the rules of procedure through which you may form the habits you desire:

First: At the beginning of the formation of a new habit put force and enthusiasm into your expression. Feel what you think. Remember that you are taking the first steps toward making the new mental path; that it is much harder at first than it will be afterwards. Make the path as clear and as deep as you can, at the beginning, so that you can readily see it the next time you wish to follow it.

Second: Keep your attention firmly concentrated on the new path-building, and keep your mind away from the old paths, lest you incline toward them. Forget all about the old paths, and concern yourself only with the new ones that you are building to order.

Third: Travel over your newly made paths as often as possible. Make opportunities for doing so, without waiting for them to arise through luck or chance. The oftener you go over the new paths the sooner will they become well worn and easily traveled. Create plans for passing over these new habit-paths, at the very start.

Fourth: Resist the temptation to travel over the older, easier paths that you have been using in the past. Every time you resist a temptation, the stronger do you become, and the easier will it be for you to do so the next time. But every time you yield to the temptation, the easier does it become to yield again, and the more difficult it becomes to resist the next time. You will have a fight on at the start, and this is the critical time. Prove your determination, persistency and will-power now, at the very beginning.

Fifth: Be sure that you have mapped out the right path, as your definite chief aim, and then go ahead without fear and without allowing yourself to doubt. "Place your hand upon the plow, and look not backward." Select your goal, then make good, deep, wide mental paths leading straight to it.

As you have already observed, there is a close relationship between habit and Auto-suggestion (self-suggestion). Through habit, an act repeatedly performed in the same manner has a tendency to become Permanent, and eventually we come to perform the act automatically or unconsciously. In playing a piano, for example, the artist can play a familiar piece while his or her conscious mind is on some other subject.

Auto-suggestion is the tool with which we dig a mental path; Concentration is the hand that holds that tool; and Habit is the map or blueprint which themental path follows. An idea or desire, to be transformed into terms of action or physical reality, must be held in the conscious mind faithfully and persistently until habit begins to give it permanent form.

Let us turn our attention, now, to environment.

As we have already seen, we absorb the material for thought from our surrounding environment. The term "environment" covers a very broad field. It consists of the books we read, the people with whom we associate, the community in which we live, the nature of the work in which we are engaged, the country or nation in which we reside, the clothes we wear, the songs we sing, and, most important of all, the religious and intellectual training we receive prior to the age of fourteen years.

The purpose of analyzing the subject of environment is to show its direct relationship to the personality we are developing, and the importance of so guarding it that its influence will give us the materials out of which we may attain our definite chief aim in life.

The mind feeds upon that which we supply it, or that which is forced upon it, through our environment; therefore, let us select our environment, as far as possible, with the object of supplying the mind with suitable material out of which to carry on its work of attaining our definite chief aim.

If your environment is not to your liking, change it!

The first step is to create in your own mind an exact, clear and well rounded out picture of the environment in which you believe you could best attain your definite chief aim, and then concentrate your mind upon this picture until you transform it into reality.

In Lesson Two, of this course, you learned that the first step you must take, in the accomplishment of any desire, is to create in your mind a dear, well defined picture of that which you intend to accomplish. This is the first principle to be observed in your plans for the achievement of success, and if you fail or neglect to observe it, you cannot succeed, except by chance.

Your daily associates constitute one of the most important and influential parts of your environment, and may work for your progress or your retrogression, according to the nature of those associates. As far as possible, you should select as your most intimate daily associates those who are in sympathy with your aims and ideals - especially those represented by your definite chief aim - and whose mental attitude inspires you with enthusiasm, self-confidence, determination and ambition.

9

Remember that every word spoken within your hearing, every sight that reaches your eyes, and every sense impression that you receive through any of the five senses, influences your thought as surely as the sun rises in the east and sets in the west. This being true, can you not see the importance of controlling, as far as possible, the environment in which you live and work? Can you not see the importance of reading books that deal with subjects which are directly related to your definite chief aim? Can you not see the importance of talking with people who are in sympathy with your aims, and, who will encourage you and spur you on toward their attainment?

We are living in what we call a "twentiethcentury civilization." The leading scientists of the world are agreed that Nature has been millions of years in creating, through the process of evolution, our present civilized environment.

How many hundreds of centuries the so-called Indians had lived upon the North American continent, without any appreciable advance toward modem civilization, as we understand it, we have no way of ascertaining. Their environment was the wilderness, and they made no attempt whatsoever to change or improve that environment; the change took place only after new races from afar came over and forced upon them the environment of progressive civilization in, which we are living today.

Observe what has happened within the short period of three centuries. Hunting grounds have been transformed into great cities, and the Indian has taken on education and culture, in many instances, that equal the accomplishment of his white brothers. (In Lesson Fifteen, we discuss the effects of environment from a worldwide viewpoint, and describe, in detail, the principal of social heredity which is the chief source through which the effects of environment may be imposed upon the minds of the young.)

The clothes you wear influence you; therefore, they constitute a part of your environment. Soiled or shabby clothes depress you and lower your self-confidence, while clean clothes, of an appropriate style, have just the opposite effect.

It is a well known fact that an observant person can accurately analyze a man by seeing his work-bench, desk or other place of employment. A well organized desk indicates a well organized brain. Showme the merchant's stock of goods and I will tell you whether he has an organized or disorganized brain, as there is a

10

close relationship between one's mental attitude and one's physical environment.

The effects of environment so vitally influence those who work in factories, stores and offices, that employers are gradually realizing the importance of creating an environment that inspires and encourages the workers.

One unusually progressive laundryman, in the city of Chicago, has plainly outdone his competitors, by installing in his work-room a player-piano, in charge of a neatly dressed young woman who keeps it going during the working hours. His laundrywomen are dressed in white uniforms, and there is no evidence about the place that work is drudgery. Through the aid of this pleasant environment, this laundryman turns out more work, earns more profits, and pays better wages than his competitors can pay.

This brings us to an appropriate place at which to describe the method through which you may apply the principles directly and indirectly related to the subject of concentration.

Let us call this method the -

MAGIC KEY TO SUCCESS!

In presenting you with this "Magic Key" let me first explain that it is no invention or discovery of mine.

It is the same key that is used, in one form or another, by the followers of New Thought and all other sects which are founded upon the positive philosophy of optimism.

This Magic Key constitutes an irresistible power which all who will may use.

It win unlock the door to riches!

It will unlock the door to fame!

And, in many instances, it will unlock the door to physical health.

It will unlock the door to education and let you into the storehouse of all your latent ability. It will act as a pass-key to any position in life for which you are fitted.

Through the aid of this Magic Key we have unlocked the secret doors to all of the world's great inventions.

Through its magic powers all of our great geniuses of the past have been developed.

Suppose you are a laborer, in a menial position, and desire a better place in life. The Magic Key will help you attain it! Through its use Carnegie, Rockefeller, Hill, Harriman, Morgan and scores of others of their type have accumulated vast fortunes of material wealth.

It will unlock prison doors and turn human derelicts into useful, trustworthy human beings. It will turn failure into success and misery into happiness.

You ask - "What is this Magic Key?"

And I answer with one word - concentration!

Now let me define concentration in the sense that it is here used. First, I wish it to be clearly understood that I have no reference to occultism, although I will admit that all the scientists of the world have failed to explain the strange phenomena produced through the aid of concentration.

Concentration, in the sense in which it is here used, means the ability, through fixed habit and practice, to keep your mind on one subject until youhave thoroughly familiarized yourself with that subject and mastered it. It means the ability to control your attention and focus it on a given problem until you have solved it.

It means the ability to throw off the effects of habits which you wish to discard, and the power to build new habits that are more to your liking. It means complete self-mastery.

Stating it in another way, concentration is the ability to think as you wish to think; the ability to control your thoughts and direct them to a definite end; and the ability to organize your knowledge into a plan of action that is sound and workable.

You can readily see that in concentrating your mind upon your definite chief aim in life, you must cover many closely related subjects which blend into each other and complete the main subject upon which you are concentrating.

Ambition and desire are the chief factors which enter into the act of successful concentration. Without these factors the Magic Key is useless, and the main reason why so few people make use of this key is that most people lack ambition, and desire nothing in particular.

Desire whatever you may, and if your desire is within reason and if it is strong enough the Magic Key of concentration will help you attain it. There are learned men of science who would have us believe that the wonderful power of prayer operates through the principle of concentration on the attainment of a deeply seated desire.

Nothing was ever created by a human being which was not first created in the imagination, throughdesire, and then transformed into reality through concentration.

Now, let us put the Magic Key to a test, through the aid of a definite formula.

First, you must put your foot on the neck of skepticism and doubt! No unbeliever ever enjoyed the benefits of this Magic Key. You must believe in the test that you are about to make.

We will assume that you have thought something about becoming a successful writer, or a powerful public speaker, or a successful business executive, or an able financier. We will take public speaking as the subject of this test, but remember that you must follow instructions to the letter.

Take a plain sheet of paper, ordinary letter size, and write on it the following:

I am going to become a powerful public speaker because this will enable me to render the world useful service that is needed - and because it will yield me a financial return that will provide me with the necessary material things of life.

I will concentrate my mind upon this desire for ten minutes daily, just before retiring at night and just after arising in the morning, for the purpose of determining just how I shall proceed to transform it into reality.

I know that I can become a powerful and magnetic speaker, therefore I will permit nothing to interfere with my doing so.

(Signed...................................................

Sign this pledge, then proceed to do as you havepledged your word that you would do. Keep it up until the desired results have been realized.

Now, when you come to do your concentrating, this is the way to go about it: Look ahead one, three, five or even ten years, and see yourself as the most powerful speaker of your time. See, in your imagination, an appropriate income. See yourself in your own home that you have purchased with the proceeds from your efforts as a speaker or lecturer. See yourself in possession of a nice bank account as a reserve for old age. See yourself as a person of influence, due to your great ability as a public speaker. See yourself engaged in a life-calling in which you will not fear the loss of your position.

Paint this picture clearly, through the powers of your imagination, and lo! it will soon become transformed into a beautiful picture of deeply seated desire. Use this desire as the chief object of your concentration and observe what happens.

You now have the secret of the Magic Key!

Do not underestimate the power of the Magic Key because it did not come to you clothed in mysticism, or because it is described in language which all who will may understand. All great truths are simple in final analysis, and easily understood; if they are not they are not great truths.

Use this Magic Key with intelligence, and only for the attainment of worthy ends, and it will bring you enduring happiness and success. Forget the mistakes you have made and the failures you-have experienced. Quit living in the past, for do you not know that your yesterdays never return? Start all over again, if your previous efforts have not turned outwell, and make the next five or ten years tell a story of success that will satisfy your most lofty ambitions.

Make a name for yourself and render the world a great service, through ambition, desire and concentrated effort!

You can do it if you BELIEVE you can!

Thus endeth the Magic Key.

. . . . . . . .

The presence of any idea or thought in your consciousness tends to produce an "associated" feeling and to urge you to appropriate or corresponding action. Hold a deeply seated desire in your consciousness, through the principle of concentration, and if you do it with full faith in its realization your act attracts to your aid powers which the entire scientific world has failed to understand or explain with a reasonable hypothesis.

When you become familiar with the powers of concentration you will then understand the reason for choosing a definite chief aim as the first step in the attainment of enduring success.

Concentrate your mind upon the attainment of the object of a deeply seated desire and very soon you will become a lode-stone that attracts, through the aid of forces which no man can explain, the necessary material counterparts of that desire, a statement of fact which paves the way for the description of a principle which constitutes the most important part of this lesson, if not, in fact, the most important part of the entire course, viz.:

When two or more people ally themselves, in a spirit of perfect harmony, for the purpose of attaining a definite end, if that alliance is faithfully observed by all of whom it is composed, the alliance brings, to each of those of whom it is composed, power that is superhuman and seemingly irresistible in nature.

Back of the foregoing statement is a law, the nature of which science has not yet determined, and it is this law that I have had in mind in connection with my repeated statements concerning the power of organized effort which you will notice throughout this course.

In chemistry we learn that two or more elements may be so compounded that the result is something entirely different in nature, from any of the individual elements. For example, ordinary water, known in chemistry under the formula of $H_2O$, is a compound consisting of two atoms of hydrogen and one atom of oxygen, but water is neither hydrogen nor oxygen. This "marrying" of elements creates an entirely different substance from that of either of its component parts.

The same law through which this transformation of physical elements takes place may be responsible for the seemingly superhuman powers resulting from the alliance of two or more people, in a perfect state of harmony and understanding, for the attainment of a given end.

This world, and all matter of which the other planets consist, is made up of electrons (an electron being the smallest known analyzable unit of matter, and resembling, in nature, what we call electricity, or a form of energy). On the other hand, thought, and that which we call the "mind," is also a form of energy; in fact it is the highest form of energy known.Thought, in other words, is organized energy, and it is not improbable that thought is exactly the same sort of energy as that which we generate with an electric dynamo, although of a much more highly organized form.

Now, if all matter, in final analysis, consists of groups of electrons, which are nothing more than a form of energy which we call electricity, and if the mind is nothing but a form of highly organized electricity, do you not see how it is possible that the laws which affect matter may also govern the mind?

And if combining two or more elements of matter, in the proper proportion and under the right conditions, will produce something entirely different from those original elements (as in the case of $H_2O$), do you not see how it is possible so to combine the energy of two or more minds that the result will be a sort of composite mind that is totally different from the individual minds of which it consists?

You have undoubtedly noticed the manner in which; you are influenced while in the presence of other people. Some people inspire you with optimism and enthusiasm. Their very presence seems to stimulate your own mind to greater action, and, this not only "seems" to be true, but it is true. You have noticed that the presence of others had a tendency to lower your vitality and depress you; a tendency which I can assure you was very real!

What, do you imagine, could be the cause of these changes that come over us when we come within a certain range of other people, unless it is the change resulting from the blending or combining of their minds with our own, through the operation of a lawthat is not very well understood, but resembles (if, in fact, it is not the same law) the law through which the combining of two atoms of hydrogen and one atom of oxygen produces water.

I have no scientific basis for this hypothesis, but I have given it many years of serious thought and always I come to the conclusion that it is at least a sound hypothesis, although I have no possible way, as yet, of reducing it to a provable hypothesis.

You need no proof, however, that the presence of some people inspires you, while the presence of others depresses you, as you know this to be a fact. Now it stands to reason that the person who inspires you and arouses your mind to a state of greater activity gives you more power to achieve, while the person whose presence depresses you and lowers your vitality, or causes you to dissipate it in useless, disorganized thought, has just the opposite effect on you. You can understand this much without the aid of a hypothesis and without further proof than that which you have experienced time after time.

Come back, now, to the original statement that:

"When two or more people ally themselves, in a spirit of perfect harmony, for the purpose of attaining a definite end, if that

16

alliance is faithfully observed by all of whom it is composed, the alliance brings, to each of those of whom it is composed, power that is superhuman and seemingly irresistible in nature."

Study, closely, the emphasized part of the foregoing statement, for there you will find the "mental formula" which, if not faithfully observed, destroys the effect of the whole.

One atom of hydrogen combined with one atom ofoxygen will not produce water, nor will an alliance in name only, that is not accompanied by "a spirit of perfect harmony" (between those forming the alliance), produce "power that is superhuman and seemingly irresistible in nature."

I have in mind a family of mountain-folk who, for more than six generations, have lived in the mountainous section of Kentucky. Generation after generation of this family came and went without any noticeable improvement of a mental nature, each generation following in the footsteps of its ancestors. They made their living from the soil, and as far as they knew, or cared, the universe consisted of a little spot of territory known as Letcher County. They married strictly in their own "set," and in their own community.

Finally, one of the members of this family strayed away from the flock, so to speak, and married a well educated and highly cultured woman from the neighbor-state of Virginia. This woman was one of those types of ambitious people who had learned that the universe extended beyond the border line of Letcher County, and covered, at least, the whole of the southern states. She had heard of chemistry, and of botany, and of biology, and of pathology, and of psychology, and of many other subjects that were of importance in the field of education. When her children began to come along to the age of understanding, she talked to them of these subjects; and they, in turn, began to show a keen interest in them.

One of her children is now the president of a great educational institution, where most of these subjects, and many others of equal importance, aretaught. Another one of them is a prominent lawyer, while still another is a successful physician.

Her husband (thanks to the influence of her mind) is a well known dental surgeon, and the first of his family, for six generations, to break away from the traditions by which the family had been bound.

The blending of her mind with his gave him the needed stimulus to spur him on and inspired him with ambition such as he would never have known without her influence.

For many years I have been studying the biographies of those whom the world calls great, and it seems to me more than a mere coincidence that in every instance where the facts were available the person who was really responsible for the greatness was in the background, behind the scenes, and seldom heard of by the hero-worshiping public. Not infrequently is this "hidden power" a patient little wife who has inspired her husband and urged him on to great achievement, as was true in the case I have just described.

Henry Ford is one of the modem miracles of this age, and I doubt that this country, or any other, ever produced an industrial genius of his equal. If the facts were known (and perhaps they are known) they might trace the cause of Mr. Ford's phenomenal achievements to a woman of whom the public hears but little - his wife!

We read of Ford's achievements and of his enormous income and imagine him to be blessed with matchless ability; and he is - ability of which the world would never have heard had it not been for the modifying influence of his wife, who has co-operated with him, during all the years of his struggle, "in a spirit of perfect harmony, for the purpose of attaining a definite end."

I have in mind another genius who is well known to the entire civilized world, Thomas A. Edison. His inventions are so well known that they need not be named. Every time you press a button and turn on an electric light, or hear a phonograph playing, you should think of Edison, for it was he who perfected both the incandescent light and the modem phonograph. Every time you see a moving picture you should think of Edison, for it was his genius, more than that of any other person, who made this great enterprise possible.

But, as in the case of Henry Ford, back of Mr. Edison stands one of the most remarkable women in America - his wife! No one outside of the Edison family, and perhaps a very few intimate personal friends of theirs, knows to what extent her influence has made Edison's achievements possible. Mrs. Edison once told me that Mr. Edison's outstanding quality, the one which, above all others, was his greatest asset, was that of -

Concentration!

When Mr. Edison starts a line of experiment or research or investigation; he never "lets go" until he either finds that for which he is looking or exhausts every possible effort to do so.

Back of Mr. Edison stand two great powers; one is concentration and the other is Mrs. Edison!

Night after night Mr. Edison has worked with such enthusiasm that he required but three or four hours of sleep. (Observe what was said about thesustaining effects of enthusiasm in Lesson Seven of this course.)

Plant a tiny apple seed in the right sort of soil, at the right time of the year, and gradually it will burst forth into a tiny sprig, and then it will expand and grow into an apple tree. That tree does not come from the soil, nor does it come from the elements of the air, but from both of these sources, and the man has not yet lived who could explain the law that attracts from the air and the soil the combination of cells of which that apple tree consists.

The tree does not come out of the tiny apple seed, but, that seed is the beginning of the tree.

When two or more people ally themselves, "in a spirit o f perfect harmony, for the purpose of attaining a definite end," the end, itself, or the desire back of that end, may be likened to the apple seed, and the blending of the forces of energy of the two or more minds may be likened to the air and the soil out of which come the elements that form the material objects of that desire.

The power back of the attraction and combination of these forces of the mind can no more be explained than can the power back of the combination of elements out of which an apple tree "grows."

But the all-important thing is that an apple tree will "grow" from a seed thus properly planted, an great achievement will follow the systematic blending of two or more minds with a definite object in view.

In Lesson Thirteen you will see this principle of allied effort carried to proportions which almost stagger the imagination of all who have not trained themselves to think in terms of organized thought!

This course, itself, is a very concrete illustrationof the principle underlying that which we have termed organized effort, but you will observe that it requires the entire sixteen lessons to complete the description of this principle. Omit a single one of the sixteen lessons and the omission would affect the whole as the removal of one link would affect the whole of a chain.

As I have already stated in many different ways, and for the purpose of emphasis, I now repeat: there is a well founded hypothesis that when one concentrates one's mind upon a given subject, facts of a nature that is closely related to that subject will "pour" in from every conceivable source. The theory is that a deeply seated desire, when once planted in the right sort of "mental soil," serves as a center of attraction or magnet that attracts to it everything that harmonizes with the nature of the desire.

Dr. Elmer Gates, of Washington, D. C., is perhaps one of the most competent psychologists in the world. He is recognized both in the field of psychology and in other directly and indirectly related fields of science, throughout the world, as being a man of the highest scientific standing.

Come with me, for a moment, and study his methods!

After Dr. Gates has followed a line of investigation as far as possible through the usual channels of research, and has availed himself of all the recorded facts at his command, on a given subject, he then takes a pencil and a tablet and "sits" for further information, by concentrating his mind on that subject until thoughts related to it begin to FLOW IN UPON HIM. He writes down these thoughts, as theycome (from he knows not where). He told me that many of his most important discoveries came through this method. It was more than twenty years ago that I first talked with Dr. Gates on this subject. Since that time, through the discovery of the radio principle, we have been provided with a reasonable hypothesis through which to explain the results of these "sittings," viz.:

The ether, as we have discovered through the modern radio apparatus, is in a constant state of agitation. Sound waves are floating through the ether at all times, but these waves cannot be detected, beyond a short distance from their source, except by the aid of properly attuned instruments.

Now, it seems reasonable to suppose that thought, being the most highly organized form of energy known, is constantly sending waves through the ether, but these waves, like those of sound, can only be detected and correctly interpreted by a properly attuned mind.

There is no doubt that when Dr. Gates sat down in a room and placed himself in a quiet, passive state of mind, the dominating thoughts in his mind served as a magnetic force that attracted the related or similar thought waves of others as they passed through the ether about him.

Taking the hypothesis just a step further, it has occurred to me many times since the discovery of the modern radio principle, that every thought that has ever been released in organized form, from the mind of any human being, is still in existence in the form of a wave in the ether, and is constantly passing around and around in a great endless circle; that the act of concentrating one's mind upon a given subject withintensity sends out thought waves which reach and blend with those of a related or similar nature, thereby establishing a direct line of communication between the one doing the concentrating and the thoughts of a similar nature which have been previously set into motion.

Going still a step further, may it not be possible for one so to attune his mind and harmonize the rate of vibration of thought with the rate of vibration of the ether that all knowledge that has been accumulated through the organized thoughts of the past is available?

With these hypotheses in mind, go back to Lesson Two, of this course, and study Carnegie's description of the "master mind" through which he accumulated his great fortune.

When Carnegie formed an alliance between more than a score of carefully selected minds, he created, by that means of compounding mind power, one of the strongest industrial forces that the world has ever witnessed. With a few notable (and very disastrous) exceptions, the men constituting the "master mind" which Carnegie created thought and acted as one!

And, that "master mind" (composed of many individual minds) was concentrated upon a single purpose, the nature of which is familiar to everyone who knew Mr. Carnegie; particularly those who were competing with him in the steel business.

If you have followed Henry Ford's record, even slightly, you undoubtedly have observed that concentrated effort has been one of the outstanding features of his career. Nearly thirty years ago he adopted a policy of standardization as to the general type of automobile that he would build, and he consistently maintained

21

that policy until. the change in public demand forced him, in 1927, to change it.

A few years ago, I met the former chief engineer of the Ford plant, and he told me of an incident that happened during the early stages of Mr. Ford's automobile experience which very clearly points to concentrated effort as being one of his prominent fundamentals of economic philosophy.

On this occasion the engineers of the Ford plant had gathered in the engineering office for the purpose of discussing a proposed change in the design of the rear axle construction of the Ford automobile. Mr. Ford stood around and listened to the discussion until each man had had his "say," then he walked over to the table, tapped the drawing of the proposed axle with his finger, and said:

"Now listen! the axle we are using does the work for which it was intended, and does it well, and there's going to be no more change in that axle!"

He turned and walked away, and from that day until this the rear axle construction of the Ford automobile has remained substantially the same. It is not improbable that Mr. Ford's success in building and marketing automobiles has been due, very largely, to his policy of consistently concentrating his efforts back of one plan, with but one definite purpose in mind at a time.

A few years ago I read Edward Bok's book, The Man From Maine, which is the biography of his father-in-law, Mr. Cyrus H. K. Curtis, the owner of the Saturday Evening Post, the Ladies' Home journal, and several other publications. All through the bookI noticed that the outstanding feature of Mr. Curtis' philosophy was that of concentration of effort back of a definite purpose.

During the early days of his ownership of the Saturday Evening Post, when he was pouring money into a losing venture by the hundreds of thousands of dollars, it required concentrated effort that was backed by courage such as but few men possess, to enable him to "carry on."

Read The Man From Maine. It is a splendid lesson on the subject of concentration, and supports, to the smallest detail, the fundamentals upon which this lesson is based.

The Saturday Evening Post is now one of the most profitable magazines in the world, but its name would have been long since forgotten had not Mr. Curtis concentrated his attention and his fortune on the one definite purpose of making it a great magazine.

down I remember it today as well as I did the day he gave it to me. This is the way that I recorded it:

The number and exchange were Lakeview 2651.

At the time he gave me the number we were standing at the railroad station, in sight of Lake Michigan; therefore, I used the lake as an associated object with which to file the name of the telephone exchange. It so happened that the telephone number was made up of the age of my brother, who was 26, and my father, who was 51, therefore I associated their names with the number, thus insuring its recall. To recall the telephone exchange and number, therefore, I had only to think of Lake Michigan, my brother and my father.

An acquaintance of mine found himself to be suffering from what is ordinarily called a "wandering mind." He was becoming "absent-minded" and unable to remember. Let him tell you, in his own words which follow, how he overcame this handicap:

"I am fifty years old. For a decade I have been a department manager in a large factory. At first my duties were easy, then the firm had a rapid expansion of business which gave me added responsibilities. Several of the young men in my department developed unusual energy and ability - at least one of them had his eye on my job.

"I had reached the age in life when a man likes to be comfortable and, having been with the company a long time, I felt that I could safely settle back into an easy berth. The effect of this mental attitude was well nigh disastrous to my position.

"About two years ago I noticed that my power of concentration was weakening and my duties were becoming irksome. I neglected my correspondence until I looked with dread upon the formidable pile of letters; reports accumulated and subordinates were inconvenienced by the delay. I sat at my desk with my mind wandering elsewhere.

"Other circumstances showed plainly that my mind was not on my work; I forgot to attend an important meeting of the officers of the company. One of the clerks under me caught a bad mistake made in an estimate on 'a carload of goods, and, of course, saw to it that the manager learned of the incident.

"I was thoroughly alarmed at the situation! and asked for a week's vacation to think things over. I was determined to resign, or find the trouble and remedy it. A few days of earnest introspection at an out-of-the-way mountain resort convinced me that I wassuffering from a plain case of mind wandering. I was lacking in concentration; my physical and mental activities at the desk had become desultory. I was careless and shiftless and neglectful - all because my mind was not alertly on the job. When I had diagnosed my case with satisfaction to myself I next sought the remedy. I needed a complete new set of working habits, and I made a resolve to acquire them.

"With paper and pencil I outlined a schedule to cover the working day: first, the morning mail; then, the orders to be filled; dictation; conference with subordinates and miscellaneous duties; ending with a clean desk before I left.

"'How is habit formed?' I asked myself mentally. `By repetition,' came back the answer. `But I have been doing these things over and over thousands of times,' the other fellow in me protested. `True, but not in orderly concentrated fashion,' replied the echo.

"I returned to the office with mind in leash, but restless, and placed my new working schedule in force at once. I performed the same duties with the same zest and as nearly as possible at the same time every day. When my mind started to slip away I quickly brought it back.

"From a mental stimulus, created by will-power, I progressed in habit building. Day after day, I practiced concentration of thought. When I found repetition becoming comfortable, then I knew that I had won."

Your ability to train your memory, or to develop any desired habit, is a matter, solely, of being able to fix your attention on a given subject until the outlineof that subject has been thoroughly impressed upon the "sensitized plate" of your mind.

Concentration, itself, is nothing but a matter of control of the attention!

You will observe that by reading a line of print with which you are not familiar, and which you have never seen before, and then closing your eyes, you can see that line as plainly as though you were looking at it on the printed page. In reality, you are "looking at it," not on the printed page, but on the sensitized plate of your own mind. If you try this experiment and it does not work the first time it is because you did not concentrate your attention on the line closely enough! Repeat the performance a few times and finally you will succeed.

If you wish to memorize poetry, for example, you can do so very quickly by training yourself to fix your attention on the lines so closely that you can shut your eyes and see them in your mind as plainly as you see them on the printed page.

So important is this subject of control of attention that I feel impelled to emphasize it in such a way that you will not pass it by lightly. I have reserved reference to this important subject until the last, as a climax to this lesson, for the reason that I consider it, by far, the most important part of the lesson.

The astounding results experienced by those who make a practice of "crystal-gazing" are due, entirely, to their ability to fix attention upon a given subject for an unbroken period far beyond the ordinary.

Crystal-gazing is nothing but concentrated attention!

I have already hinted at that which I will nowstate as my belief, namely, that it is possible, through the aid of concentrated attention, for one so to attune one's mind to the vibration of the ether that all the secrets in the world of unfathomed and uncharted mental phenomena may become as open books which may be read at will.

What a thought this is to ponder over!

I am of the opinion, and not without substantial evidence to support me, that it is possible for one to develop the ability of fixing the attention so highly that one may "tune in" and understand that which is in the mind of any person. But this is not all, nor is it the most important part of a hypothesis at which I have arrived after many years of careful research, for I am satisfied that one may just as easily go a step further and "tune in" on the universal mind in which all knowledge is stored where it may be appropriated by all who master the art of coming after it.

To a highly orthodox mind these statements may seem very irrational; but, to the student (and, so far, there are but few people in the world who are more than mere students, of an elementary grade, of this subject) who has studied this subject with any appreciable degree of understanding, these hypotheses seem not only possible, but absolutely probable.

But put the hypothesis to a test of your own!

You can select no better subject upon which to try an experiment than that which you have selected as your definite chief aim in life.

Memorize your definite chief aim so you can repeat it without looking at the written page, then make a practice of fixing your attention on it at least twice a day, proceeding as follows:

Go into some quiet place where you will not be disturbed; sit down and completely relax your mind and your body; then close your eyes and place your fingers in your ears, thereby excluding the ordinary sound waves and all of the light waves. In that position repeat your definite chief aim in life, and as you do so see yourself, in your imagination, in full possession of the object of that aim. If a part of your aim is the accumulation of money, as it undoubtedly is, then see yourself in possession of that money. If a part of the object of your definite aim is the ownership of a home, then see a picture of that home, in your imagination, just as you expect to see it in reality. If a part of your definite aim is to become a powerful and influential public speaker, then see yourself before an enormous audience, and feel yourself playing upon the emotions of that audience as a great violinist would play upon the strings of the violin.

As you approach the end of this lesson, there are two things which you might do, viz.

First: You might begin, now, to cultivate the ability to fix attention, at will, on a given subject, with a feeling that this ability, when fully developed, would bring you the object of your definite chief aim in life; or,

Second: You might tilt your nose in the air and with the smile of a cynic say to yourself - "Bosh" and thereby mark yourself a fool!

Take your choice!

This lesson was not written as an argument, nor as the subject of a debate. It is your privilege to accept it, in whole or in part, or reject it, just as you please.

But at this place I wish to state, however, that this is not an age of cynicism or doubt. An age that has conquered the air above us and the sea beneath us, that has enabled us to harness the air and turn it into a messenger that will carry the sound of our voice half-way around the earth in the fractional part of a second, certainly is not an age that lends encouragement to the "doubting Thomases" or the "I-don't-believe-it Joneses."

The human family has passed through the "Stone Age" and the "Iron Age" and the "Steel Age," and unless I have greatly misinterpreted the trend of the times it is now entering the "Mind

Power Age," which will eclipse, in stupendous achievement, all the other "ages" combined.

Learn to fix your attention on a given subject, at will, for whatever length of time you choose, and you will have learned the secret passage-way to power and plenty!

This is concentration!

You will understand, from this lesson, that the object of forming an alliance between two or more people, and thereby creating a "Master Mind," is to apply the Law of Concentration more effectively than it could be applied through the efforts of but one person.

The principle referred to as the "Master Mind" is nothing more nor less than group concentration of mind power upon the attainment of a definite object or end. Greater power comes through group mind concentration because of the "stepping up" process Produced through the reaction of one mind upon another or others.

## PERSUASION VS. FORCE

Success, as has been stated in dozens of different ways throughout this course, is very largely a matter of tactful and harmonious negotiation with other people. Generally speaking, the man who understands how to "get people to do things" he wants done may succeed in any calling.

As a fitting climax for this lesson, on the Law of Concentration, we shall describe the principles through which men are influenced; through which cooperation is gained; through which antagonism is eliminated and friendliness developed.

Force sometimes gets what appear to be satisfactory results, but force, alone, never has built and never can build enduring success.

The world war has done more than anything which has happened in the history of the world to show us the futility of force as a means of influencing the human mind. Without going into details or recounting the instances which could be cited, we all know that force was the foundation upon which German philosophy has been built during the past forty years. The doctrine that might makes right was given a worldwide trial and it failed.

The human body can be imprisoned or controlled by physical force, but it is not so with the human mind. No man on earth can

29

control the mind of a normal, healthy person if that person chooses to exercise his God-given right to control his own mind. The majority of people do not exercise this right. They go through the world, thanks to our faulty educational system, without having discovered thestrength which lies dormant in their own minds. Now and then something happens, more in the nature of an accident than anything else, which awakens a person and causes him to discover where his real strength lies and how to use it in the development of industry or one of the professions. Result: a genius is born!

There is a given point at which the human mind stops rising or exploring unless something out of the daily routine happens to "push" it over this obstacle. In some minds this point is very low and in others it is very high. In still others it varies between low and high. The individual who discovers a way to stimulate his mind artificially, arouse it and cause it to go beyond this average stopping point frequently, is sure to be rewarded with fame and fortune if his efforts are of a constructive nature.

The educator who discovers a way to stimulate any mind and cause it to rise above this average stopping point without any bad reactionary effects, will confer a blessing on the human race second to none in the history of the world. We, of course, do not have reference to physical stimulants or narcotics. These will always arouse the mind for a time, but eventually they ruin it entirely. We have reference to a purely mental stimulant, such as that which comes through intense interest, desire, enthusiasm, love, etc., the factors out of which a "Master Mind" may be developed.

The person who makes this discovery will do much toward solving the crime problem. You can do almost anything with a person when you learn how to influence his mind. The mind may be likened to a great field. It is a very fertile field which always produces a crop after the kind of seed which is sownin it. The problem, then, is to learn how to select the right sort of seed and how to sow that seed so that it takes root and grows quickly. We are sowing seed in our minds daily, hourly, nay, every second, but we are doing it promiscuously and more or less unconsciously. We must learn to do it after a carefully prepared plan, according to a well laid out design! Haphazardly sown seed in the human mind brings back a haphazard crop! There is no escape from this result.

History is full of notable cases of men who have been transformed from law-abiding, peaceful, constructive citizens to roving, vicious criminals. We also have thousands of cases wherein men of the low, vicious, so-called criminal type have been transformed into constructive, law-abiding citizens. In every one of these cases the transformation of the human being took place in the mind of the man. He created in his own mind, for one reason or another, a picture of what, he desired and then proceeded to transform that picture into reality. As a matter of fact, if a picture of; any environment, condition or thing be pictured in the human mind and if the mind be focused or concentrated on that picture long enough and persistently enough, and backed up with a strong desire for the thing pictured, it is but a short step from the picture, to the realization of it in physical or mental form.

The world war brought out many startling tendencies of the human mind which corroborate the work which the psychologist has carried on in his research into the workings of the mind. The following account of a rough, uncouth, unschooled, undisciplined young mountaineer is an excellent case in point:

## FOUGHT FOR HIS RELIGION; NOW GREAT WAR HERO

———————

Rotarians Plan to Present Farm to Arvin York, Unlettered Tennessee Squirrel Hunter

### BY GEORGE W. DIXON

How Arvin Cullom York, an unlettered Tennessee squirrel hunter, became the foremost hero of the American Expeditionary Forces in France, forms a romantic chapter in the history of the world war.

York is a native of Fentress County. He was born and reared among the hardy mountaineers of the Tennessee woods. There is not even a railroad in Fentress County. During his earlier years he was reputed to be a desperate character. He was what was known as a gunman. He was a dead shot with a revolver, and his prowess with the rifle was known far and wide among the plain people of the Tennessee hills.

One day a religious organization pitched its tent in the community in which York and his parents lived. It was a strange sect that came to the mountains looking for converts, but the methods of the evangels of the new cult were full of fire and emotionalism. They denounced the sinner, the vile character and the man who took advantage of his neighbor. They pointed to the religion of the Master as an example that all should follow.

## ALVIN GETS RELIGION

Alvin Cullom York startled his neighbors one night by flinging himself down at the mourners' bench. Old men stirred in their seats and women craned their necks, as York wrestled with his sins in the shadows of the Tennessee mountains.

York became an ardent apostle of the new religion. He became an exhorter, a leader in the religious life of the community and, although his marksmanship was as deadly as ever, no one feared him who walked in the path of righteousness.

When the news of the war reached that remote section of Tennessee and the mountaineers were told that they were going to be "conscripted," York grew sullen and disagreeable. He didn't believe in killing human beings, even in war. His Bible taught him, "Thou shalt not kill." To his mind this was literal and final. He was branded as a "conscientious objector."

The draft officers anticipated trouble. They knew that his mind was made up, and they would have to reach him in some manner other than by threats of punishment.

## WAR IN A HOLY CAUSE

They went to York with a Bible and showed him that the war was in a holy cause - the cause of liberty and human freedom. They pointed out that men like himself were called upon by the Higher Powers to make the world free; to protect innocent women and children from violation; to make life worth living for the poor and oppressed; to overcome the "beast" pictured in the Scriptures. It was a fight between the hosts of righteousness and the hordes of Satan. Thedevil was trying to conquer the world through his chosen agents, the Kaiser and his generals.

York's eyes blazed with a fierce light. His big hands closed like a vise. His strong jaws snapped. "The Kaiser," he hissed between his teeth, "the beast! the destroyer of women and children! I'll show him where he belongs if I ever get within gunshot of him!"

He caressed his rifle, kissed his mother good-by and told her he would see her again when the Kaiser had been put out of business.

He went to the training camp and drilled with scrupulous care and strict obedience to orders.

His skill at target practice attracted attention. His comrades were puzzled at his high scores. They had not reckoned that a backwoods squirrel hunter would make fine material for a sniper in the front-line trenches.

York's part in the war is now history. General Pershing has designated him as the foremost individual hero of the war. He won every decoration, including the Congressional Medal, the Croix de Guerre, the Legion of Honor. He faced the Germans without fear of death. He was fighting to vindicate his religion, for the sanctity of the home; the love of women and children. Fear was not in his code or his vocabulary. His cod daring electrified more than a million men and set the world to talking about this strange, unlettered hero from the hills of Tennessee.

Here we have a case of a young mountaineer who, had he been approached from just a slightly different angle, undoubtedly would have resisted conscriptionand, likely as not, would have become so embittered toward his country that he would have become an outlaw, looking for an opportunity to strike back at the first chance.

Those who approached him knew something of the principles through which the human mind works. They knew how to manage young York by first overcoming the resistance that he had worked up in his own mind. This is the very point at which thousands of men, through improper understanding of these principles, are arbitrarily classed as criminals and treated as dangerous, vicious people. Through suggestion these people could have been handled as effectively as young York was handled, and developed into useful, productive human beings.

In your search for ways and means of understanding and manipulating your own mind so you can persuade it to create that which you desire in life, let us remind you that, without a single exception, anything which irritates you and arouses you to anger, hatred, dislike, or cynicism, is destructive and very bad for you.

You can never get the maximum or even a fair average of constructive action out of your mind until you have learned to control it and keep it from becoming stimulated through anger or fear!

These two negatives, anger and fear, are positively destructive to your mind, and as long as you allow them to remain you can be sure of results which are unsatisfactory and away below what you are capable of producing.

In our discussion of environment and habit we learned that the individual mind is amenable to thesuggestions of environment; that the minds of the individuals of a crowd blend with one another conforming to the suggestion of the prevailing influence of the leader or dominating figure. Mr. J. A. Fisk gives us an interesting account of the influence of mental suggestion in the revival meeting, which bears out the statement that the crowd mind blends into one, as follows:

MENTAL SUGGESTION IN THE REVIVAL

Modern psychology has firmly established the fact that the greater part of the phenomena of the religious "revival" are psychical rather than spiritual in their nature, and abnormally psychical at that. The leading authorities recognize the fact that the mental excitement attendant upon the emotional appeals of the "revivalist" must be classified with the phenomena, of hypnotic suggestion rather than with that of true, religious experience. And those who have made a close study of the subject believe that instead of such excitement tending to elevate the mind and exalt the spirit of the individual, it serves to weaken and degrade the mind and prostitute the spirit by dragging it in the mud of abnormal psychic frenzy and emotional excess. In fact, by some careful observers, familiar with the respective phenomena, the religious "revival" meeting is classed with the public hypnotic "entertainment" as a typical example of psychic intoxication and hysterical excess.

David Starr Jordan, chancellor emeritus of Leland Stanford University, says: "Whisky, cocaine and alcohol bring temporary insanity, and so does a revival of religion." The late Professor

WilliamJames, of Harvard University, the eminent psychologist, says: "Religious revivalism is more dangerous to the life of society than drunkenness."

It should be unnecessary to state that in this lesson the term "revival" is used in the narrower signification indicating the typical religious emotional excitement known by the term in question, and is not intended to apply to the older and respected religious experience designated by the same term, which was so highly revered among the Puritans, Lutherans and others in the past.

In order to understand the principle of the operation of mental suggestion in the revival meeting, we must first understand something of what is known as the psychology of the crowd. Psychologists are aware that the psychology of a crowd, considered as a whole, differs materially from that of the separate individuals composing that crowd. There is a crowd of separate individuals, and a composite crowd in which the emotional natures of the units seem to blend and fuse. The change from the first-named crowd to the second arises from the influence of earnest attention, or deep emotional appeals or common interest. Whenthis change occurs the crowd becomes a composite individual, the degree of whose intelligence and emotional control is but little above that of its weakest member. This fact, startling as it may appear to the average reader, is well known and is admitted by the leading psychologists of the day; and many important essays and books have been written thereupon. The predominant characteristics of this "composite-mindedness" of a crowd are the evidences of extreme suggestibility, response to appeals of emotion, vivid imagination, and action arising from imitation - all of which are mental traits universally manifested by primitive man. In short, the crowd manifests atavism, or reversion to early racial traits.

Dials, in his Psychology of the Aggregate Mind of an Audience, holds that the mind of an assemblage listening to a powerful speaker undergoes a curious process called "fusion," by which the individuals in the audience, losing their personal traits for the time being, to a greater or less degree, are reduced, as it were, to a single individual, whose characteristics are those of an impulsive youth of twenty, imbued in general with high ideals, but sacking in reasoning. power and will. Tarde, the French psychologist, advances similar views.

Professor Joseph Jastrow, in his Fact and Fable in Psychology, says:

"In the production of this state of mind a factor as yet unmentioned plays a leading rôle, the power of mental contagion. Error, like truth, flourishes in crowds. At the heart of sympathy each finds a home... No form of contagion is so insidious in its outset, so difficult to check in its advance, so certain to leavegerms that may at any moment reveal their pernicious power, as a mental contagion - the contagion of fear, of panic, of fanaticism, of lawlessness, of superstition, of error....In brief, we must add to the many factors which contribute to deception, the recognized lowering of critical ability, of the power of accurate observation, indeed, of rationality, which merely being one of a crowd induces. The conjurer finds it easy to perform to a large audience, because, among other reasons, it is easier to arouse their admiration and sympathy, easier to make them forget themselves and enter into the uncritical spirit of wonderland. It would seem that in some respects the critical tone of an assembly, like the strength of a chain, is that of its weakest member."

Professor Le Bon, in his The Crowd, says:

"The sentiments and ideas of all the persons in the gathering take one and the same direction, and their conscious personality vanishes. A collective mind is formed, doubtless transitory, by presenting very clearly marked characteristics. The gathering has become what, in the absence of a better expression, I will call an organized crowd, or, if the term be considered preferable, a psychological crowd. It forms a single being, and is subjected to the law of the mental unity of crowds....The most striking peculiarity presented by a psychological crowd is the following: Whoever be the individuals that compose it, however like or unlike be their mode of life, their occupation, their character, or their intelligence, the fact that they have been transformed into a crowd puts them in Possession of a sort of collective mind which makes them feel, think and act in a manner quite differentfrom that in which each individual of them would feel, think and act were he in a state of isolation. There are certain ideas and feelings which do not come into being, or do not transform themselves into acts, except in the case of the individuals forming a crowd....In crowds it is stupidity and not mother wit that is accumulated. In the collective mind the intellectual aptitudes of the individuals, and in consequence their individuality, is weakened....The most careful observations seem to prove that an individual immerged for some length of time in a crowd in action soon finds himself in a special state, which most resembles the state of fascination in which the hypnotized individual finds himself....The conscious personality has entirely vanished, will and discernment are lost. All feelings and thoughts are bent in the direction determined by the hypnotizer....Under the influence of a suggestion he will undertake the accomplishment of certain acts with irresistible impetuosity. This impetuosity is the more irresistible in the case of crowds, from the fact that, the suggestion being the same for all the individuals of the crowd, it gains in strength by reciprocity. Moreover, by the mere fact that he forms part of an organized crowd, a man descends several rungs in the ladder of civilization. Isolated, he may be a cultured individual; in a crowd, he is a barbarian - that is, a creature acting by instinct. He possesses the spontaneity, the violence, the ferocity, and also the enthusiasm and heroism of primitive beings, whom he further tends to resemble by the facility with which he allows himself to be induced to commit acts contrary to his most obvious interests and his best known habits. An individual in a crowd is a grain of sandamid other grains of sand, which the wind stirs up at will."

Professor Davenport, in his Primitive Traits in Religious Revivals, says:

"The mind of the crowd is strangely like that of primitive man. Most of the people in it may be far from primitive in emotion, in thought, in character; nevertheless, the result tends always to be the same. Stimulation immediately begets action. Reason is in abeyance. The cool, rational speaker has little chance beside the skillful emotional orator. The crowd thinks in images, and speech must take this form to be accessible to it. The images are not connected by any natural bond, and they take each other's place like the slides of a magic lantern. It follows from this, of course, that appeals to the imagination have paramount influence....The crowd is united and governed by emotion rather than by reason. Emotion is the natural bond, for men differ much less in this respect than in intellect. It is also true that in a crowd of a thousand men the amount of emotion actually generated and existing is far greater than the sum which might conceivably be obtained by adding together the emotions of the individuals taken by themselves. The explanation of this is that the attention of the crowd is always directed either by the circumstances of the occasion or by the speaker to certain common ideas - as 'salvation' in religious gatherings....and every individual in the gathering is stirred with emotion, not only because the idea or the shibboleth stirs him, but also because he is conscious that every other individual in the gathering believes in the idea or the shibboleth, and is stirred by it, too. And this enormously increases the volume of his own emotion and consequently the total volume of emotion in the crowd. As in the case of the primitive mind, imagination has unlocked the floodgates of emotion, which on occasion may become wild enthusiasm or demoniac frenzy."

The student of suggestion will see that not only are the emotional members of a revival audience subject to the effect of the "composite-mindedness" arising from the "psychology of the crowd" and are thereby weakened in resistive power, but that they are also brought under the influence of two other very potent forms of mental suggestion. Added to the powerful suggestion of authority exercised by the revivalist, which is exerted to its fullest along lines very similar to that of the professional hypnotist, is the suggestion of imitation exerted upon each individual by the combined force of the balance of the crowd.

As Durkheim observed in his psychological investigations, the average individual is "intimidated by the mass" of the crowd around him, or before him, and experiences that peculiar psychological influence exerted by the mere number of people as against his individual self. Not only does the suggestible person find it easy to respond to the authoritative suggestions of the preacher and the exhortations of his helpers, but he is also brought under the direct fire of the imitative suggestions of those on all sides who are experiencing emotional activities and who are manifesting them outwardly. Not only does the voice of the shepherd urge forward, but the tinkle of the bellwether's bell is also heard, and the imitative tendency of the flock, which causes one sheep to jumpbecause one ahead of him does so (and so on until the last sheep has jumped), needs but the force of the example of a leader to start into motion the entire flock. This is not an exaggeration - human beings, in times of panic, fright, or deep emotion of any kind, manifest the imitative tendency of the sheep, and the tendency of cattle and horses to "stampede" under imitation.

To the student experienced in the experimental work of the psychological laboratory there is the very closest analogy observed in the respective phenomena of the revival and hypnotic suggestion. In both cases the attention and interest is attracted by the unusual procedure; the element of mystery and awe is induced by words and actions calculated to inspire them; the senses are tired by monotonous talk in an impressive and authoritative tone; and finally the suggestions are projected in a commanding, suggestive manner familiar to all students of hypnotic suggestion. The subjects in both cases are prepared for the final suggestions and commands, by previously given minor suggestions, such as: "Stand up," or "Look this way," etc., in the case of the hypnotist; and by: "All those who think so-and-so, stand up," and "All who are willing to become better, stand up," etc., in the case of the revivalist. The impressionable subjects are thus accustomed to obedience to suggestion by easy stages. And, finally, the commanding suggestion: "Come right up - right up - this way - right up - come, I say, come, come, COME! " etc., which takes the impressed ones right off their feet and rushes them to the front, are, almost precisely the same in the hypnotic experiment or séance, on the one hand, and the sensational revival, on the other. Every good revivalist wouldmake a good hypnotic operator, and every good hypnotic operator would make a good revivalist if his mind were turned in that direction.

In the revival, the person giving the suggestions has the advantage of breaking down the resistance of his audience by arousing their sentiments and emotions. Tales depicting the influence of mother, home and heaven; songs like "Tell Mother, I'll Be There"; and personal appeals to the revered associations of one's past and early life tend to reduce one to the state of emotional response, and render him most susceptible to strong, repeated suggestions along the same line. Young people and hysterical women are especially susceptible to this form of emotional suggestion. Their feelings are stirred, and the will is influenced by the preaching, the songs, and the personal appeals of the co-workers of the revivalist.

The most sacred sentimental memories are reawakened for the moment and old conditions of mind are reinduced. "Where Is My Wandering Boy Tonight?" brings forth tears to many a one to whom the memory of the mother is sacred, and the preaching that the mother is dwelling in a state of bliss beyond the skies, from which the unconverted child is cut off unless he professes faith, serves to move many to action for the time being. The element of fear is also invoked in the revival - not so much as formerly, it is true, but still to a considerable extent and more subtly. The fear of a sudden death in an unconverted condition is held over the audience, and, "Why not now - why not tonight?" is asked him, accompanied by the hymn; "Oh, Why Do You Wait, Dear Brother?" As Davenport says:

"It is well known that the employment of symbolic images immensely increases the emotion of an audience. The vocabulary of revivals abounds in them - the cross, the crown, the angel band, hell, heaven. Now vivid imagination and strong feeling and belief are states of mind favorable to suggestion as well as to impulsive action. It is also true that the influence of a crowd largely in sympathy with the ideas suggested is thoroughly coercive or intimidative upon the individual sinner. There is considerable professed conversion which results in the beginning from little more than this form of social pressure, and which may never develop beyond it. Finally, the inhibition of all extraneous ideas is encouraged in revival assemblies both by prayer and speech. There is, therefore, extreme sensitiveness to suggestion. When to these conditions of negative consciousness on the part of an audience there has been added a conductor of the meetings who has a high hypnotic potential, such as Wesley or Finney, or who is only a thoroughly persuasive and magnetic personality, such as Whitefield, there may easily be an influence exerted upon certain individuals of a crowd which closely approaches the abnormal or thoroughly hypnotic. When this point is not reached there is still a great amount of highly acute though normal suggestibility to be reckoned with."

The persons who show signs of being influenced are then "labored with" by either the revivalist or his co-workers. They are urged to surrender their will, and "Leave it all to the Lord." They are told to "Give yourself to God, now, right now, this minute"; or to "Only believe now, and you shall be saved" etc. They are exhortedand prayed with; arms are placed around their shoulders, and every art of emotional persuasive suggestion is used to make the sinner "give up."

Starbuck in his The Psychology of Religion relates a number of instances of the experiences of converted persons at revivals. One person wrote as follows:

"My will seemed wholly at the mercy of others, particularly of the revivalist M_. There was absolutely no intellectual element. It was pure feeling. There followed a period of ecstasy. I was bent on doing good and was eloquent in appealing to others. The state of moral exaltation did not continue. It was followed by a complete relapse from orthodox religion."

Davenport has the following to say in reply to the claim that the old methods of influencing converts at a revival have passed away with the crude theology of the past:

"I lay particular stress upon this matter here, because, while the employment of irrational fear in revivals has largely passed away, the employment of the hypnotic method has not passed away. There has rather been a recrudescence and a conscious strengthening of it because the old prop of terror is gone. And it cannot be too vigorously emphasized that such a force is not a 'spiritual' force in any high and clear sense at all, but is rather uncanny and psychic and obscure. And the method itself needs to be greatly refined before it can ever be of any spiritual benefit whatever. It is thoroughly primitive and belongs with the animal and instinctive means of fascination. In this bald, crude form, the feline employs it upon the helpless bird and the Indian medicine-man upon the ghost-dance votary. When used, as it has often been, upon little children who are naturally highly suggestible, it has no justification whatever and is mentally and morally injurious in the highest degree. I do not see how violent emotional throes and the use of suggestion in its crude forms can be made serviceable even in the cases of hardened sinners, and certainly with large classes of the population the employment of this means is nothing but psychological malpractice. We guard with intelligent care against quackery in physiological obstetrics. It would be well if a sterner training and prohibition hedged about the spiritual obstetrician, whose function it is to guide the far more delicate process of the new birth."

Some who favor the methods of the revival, but who also recognize the fact that mental suggestion plays a most important part in the phenomena thereof, hold that the objections similar to those here advanced are not valid against the methods of the revival, inasmuch as mental suggestion, as is well known, may be used for good purposes as well as bad - for the benefit and uplifting of people as well as in the opposite direction. This being admitted, these good folks argue that mental suggestion in the revival is a legitimate method or "weapon of attack upon the stronghold of the devil." But this argument is found to be defective when examined in its effects and consequences. In the first place, it would seem to identify the emotional, neurotic and hysterical mental states induced by revival methods with the spiritual uplift and moral regeneration which is the accompaniment of true religious experience. It seeks to place the counterfeit on a par with the genuine - the  baleful glare of the rays of the psychic moon with the invigorating and animating rays of the spiritual sun. It seeks to raise the hypnotic phase to that of the "spiritual-mindedness" of man. To those who are familiar with the two classes of phenomena, there is a difference as wide as that between the poles existing between them.

But what do the authorities say of the revival of the future - the new revival - the real revival? LetProfessor Davenport speak for the critics - he is well adapted for the task. He says:

"There will be, I believe, far less use of the revival meeting as a crass coercive instrument for overriding the will and overwhelming the reason of the individual man. The influence of public religious gatherings will be more indirect, more unobtrusive. It will be recognized that hypnotization and forced choices weaken the soul, and there will be no attempt to press to decision in so great a matter under the spell of excitement and contagion and suggestion. . . . The converts may be few. They may be many. They will be measured, not by the capacity of the preacher for administrative hypnotism, but rather by the capacity for unselfish friendship of every man and woman. But of this I think we may be confident - the days of religious effervescence and passional unrestraint are dying. The days of intelligent, undemonstrative and self-sacrificing piety are dawning. To do justly, to love mercy, to walk humbly with God - these remain the cardinal tests of the divine in man.

Religious experience is an evolution. We go on from the rudimentary and the primitive to the rational and the spiritual. And, believe Paul, the mature fruit of the Spirit is not the subliminal uprush, the lapse of inhibition, but rational love, joy, peace, long-suffering, kindness, goodness, faithfulness, meekness - self-control."

. . . . . . . .

The Law of Concentration is one of the major principles which must be understood and applied intelligently by all who would successfully experiment with the principle described in this course as the "Master Mind."

The foregoing comments, by leading authorities of the world, will give you a better understanding of the Law of Concentration as it is often used by those who wish to "blend" or "fuse" the minds of a crowd so they will function as a single mind.

You are now ready for the lesson on Co-operation, which will take you further into the methods of applying the psychological laws upon which this philosophy of success is based.

# Lesson Thirteen

## CO-OPERATION

### "You Can Do It if You Believe You Can!"

CO-OPERATION is the beginning of all organized effort. As was stated in the second lesson of this course, Andrew Carnegie accumulated a gigantic fortune through the co-operative efforts of a small group of men numbering not more than a score.

You, too, can learn how to use this principle.

There are two forms of Co-operation to which your attention will be directed in this lesson; namely:

First, the Co-operation between people who group themselves together or form alliances for the purpose of attaining a given end, under the principles known as the Law of the Master Mind.

Second, the Co-operation between the conscious and the subconscious minds, which forms a reasonable hypothesis of man's ability to contact, communicate with and draw upon infinite intelligence.

To one who has not given serious thought to this subject, the foregoing hypothesis may seem unreasonable; but follow the evidence of itssoundness, and study the facts upon which the hypothesis is based, and then draw your own conclusions.

Let us begin with a brief review of the physical construction of the body:

"We know that the whole body is traversed by a network of nerves which serve as the channels of communication between the indwelling spiritual ego, which we call mind, and the functions of the external organism.

"This nervous system is dual. One system, known as the Sympathetic, is the channel for all those activities which are not consciously directed by our volition, such as the operation of the digestive organs, the repair of the daily wear and tear of the tissues, and the like.

"The other system, known as the Voluntary or Cerebro-spinal system, is the channel through which we receive conscious perception from the physical senses and exercise control over the movements of the body. This system has its center in the brain,

45

while the other has its center in the ganglionic mass at the back of the stomach known as the solar plexus, and sometimes spoken of as the abdominal brain. The cerebro-spinal system is the channel of our volitional or conscious mental action, and the sympathetic system is the channel of that mental action which unconsciously supports the vital functions of the body.

"Thus the cerebro-spinal system is the organ of the conscious mind and the sympathetic is that of the subconscious mind.

"But the interaction of conscious and sub-conscious minds requires a similar interaction between the corresponding systems of nerves, and one conspicuous connection by which this is provided is the "vagus" nerve. This nerve passes out of the cerebral region as a portion of the voluntary system, and through it we control the vocal organs; then it passes onward to the thorax, sending out branches to the heart and lungs; and finally, passing through the diaphragm, it loses the outer coating which distinguishes the nerves of the voluntary system and becomes identified with those of the sympathetic system, so forming a connecting link between the two and making the man physically a single entity.

"Similarly different areas of the brain indicate their connection with the objective and subjective activities of the mind respectively, and, speaking in a general way, we may assign the frontal portion of the brain to the former, and the posterior portion to the latter, while the intermediate portion partakes of the character of both.

"The intuitional faculty has its correspondence in the upper area of the brain, situated between the frontal and the posterior portions, and, physiologically speaking, it is here that intuitive ideas find entrance. These, at first, are more or less unformed and generalized in character, but are, nevertheless, perceived by the conscious mind; otherwise, we should not be aware of them at all. Then the effort of Nature is to bring these ideas into more definite and usable shape, so the conscious mind lays hold on them and induces a corresponding vibratory current in the voluntary system of nerves, and this in turn induces a similar current in the involuntary system, thus handing the idea over to the subjective mind. The vibratory current which had first descendedfrom the apex of the brain to the frontal brain and thus through the voluntary system to the solar plexus is now reversed and ascends from the solar plexus through the sympathetic system to the posterior brain, this return current indicating the action of the subjective mind."

If we were to remove the surface portion of the apex of the brain we should find immediately below it the shining belt of brain substance called the "corpus callous." This is the point of union between the subjective and objective, and, as the current returns from the solar plexus to this point, it is restored to the objective portion of the brain in a fresh form which it has acquired by the silent alchemy of the subjective mind. Thus the conception which was at first only vaguely recognized is restored to the objective mind in a definite and workable form, and then the objective mind, acting through the frontal brain - the area of comparison and analysis - proceeds to work upon a clearly perceived idea and to bring out the potentialities that are latent in it[1].

The term "subjective mind" is the same as the term "sub-conscious mind," and the term "objective mind" is the same as the term "conscious mind."

Please understand these different terms.

By studying this dual system through which the body transmits energy, we discover the exact points at which the two systems are connected, and the manner in which we may transmit a thought from the conscious to the subconscious mind.

This Co-operative dual nervous system is the most important form of co-operation known to man; for it is through the aid of this system that the principle of evolution carries on its work of developing accurate thought, as described in Lesson Eleven.

When you impress any idea on your sub-conscious mind, through the principle of Auto-suggestion, you do so with the aid of this dual nervous system: and when your sub-conscious mind works out a definite plan of any desire with which you impress it, the plan is delivered back to your conscious mind through this same dual nervous system.

This Co-operative system of nerves literally constitutes a direct line of communication between your ordinary conscious mind and infinite intelligence.

---

[1]Judge T. Toward, in The Edinburgh Lectures on Mental Science.

Knowing, from my own previous experience as a beginner in the study of this subject, how difficult it is to accept the hypothesis here described, I will illustrate the soundness of the hypothesis in a simple way that you can both understand and demonstrate for yourself.

Before going to sleep at night impress upon your mind the desire to arise the next morning at a given hour, say at four A.M., and if your impression is accompanied by a positive determination to arise at that hour, your sub-conscious mind will register the impression and awaken you at precisely that time.

Now the question might well be asked:

"If I ran impress my sub-conscious mind with the desire to arise at a specified time and it will awaken me at that time, why do I not form the habit of impressing it with other and more important desires?"

If you will ask yourself this question, and insist upon an answer, you will find yourself very near, if not on the pathway that leads to the secret door to knowledge, as described in Lesson Eleven.

. . . . . . . .

We will now take up the subject of Co-operation between men who unite, or group themselves together for the purpose of attaining a given end. In the second lesson of this course we referred to this sort of cooperation as organized effort.

This course touches some phase of co-operation in practically every lesson. This result was inevitable for the reason that the object of the course is to help the student develop power, and power is developed only through organized effort.

We are living in an age of co-operative effort. Nearly all successful businesses are conducted under some form of co-operation. The same is true in the field of industry and finance, as well as in the professional field.

Doctors and lawyers have their alliances for mutual aid and protection in the form of Bar Associations and Medical Associations.

The bankers have both local and national Associations for their mutual aid and advancement.

The retail merchants have their Associations for the same purpose. The automobile owners have grouped themselves into Clubs and Associations.

The Printers have their Associations; the plumbers have theirs and the coal dealers have theirs.

Co-operation is the object of all these Associations.

The laboring men have their unions and those who supply the working capital and superintend theefforts of laboring men have their alliances, under various names.

Nations have their co-operative alliances, although they do not appear to have yet discovered the full meaning of "co-operation." The attempt of the late President Wilson to perfect the League of Nations, followed by the efforts of the late President Harding to perfect the same idea under the name of the World Court, indicates the trend of the times in the direction of co-operation.

It is slowly becoming obvious to man that those who most efficiently apply the principle of co-operative effort survive longest, and, that this principle applies from the lowest form of animal life to the highest form of human endeavor.

Mr. Carnegie, and Mr. Rockefeller, and Mr. Ford have taught the business man the value of co-operative effort; that is, they have taught all who cared to observe, the principle through which they accumulated vast fortunes.

Co-operation is the very foundation of all successful leadership. Henry Ford's most tangible asset is the well organized agency force that he has established. This organization not only provides him with an outlet for all the automobiles he can manufacture, but, of greater importance still, it provides him with financial power sufficient to meet any emergency that may arise, a fact which he has already demonstrated on at least one occasion.

As a result of his understanding of the value of the co-operative principle Ford has removed himself from the usual position of dependence upon financial institutions and at the same time provided himselfwith more commercial power than he can possibly use.

The Federal Reserve Bank System is another example of co-operative effort which practically insures the United States against a money panic.

The chain-store systems constitute another form of commercial co-operation that provides advantage through both the purchasing and the distributing end of the business.

The modern department store, which is the equivalent of a group of small stores operating under one roof, one management and one overhead expense, is another illustration of the advantage of co-operative effort in the commercial field.

In Lesson Fifteen you will observe the possibilities of co-operative effort in its highest form and at the same time you will see the important part that it plays in the development of power.

As you have already learned, power is organized effort. The three most important factors that enter into the process of organizing effort are:

Concentration,

Co-operation and

Co-ordination.

## HOW POWER IS DEVELOPED THROUGH CO-OPERATION

As we have already seen, power is organized effort or energy. Personal power is developed by developing, organizing and co-ordinating the faculties of the mind. This may be accomplished by mastering and applying the fifteen major principles upon which this course is founded. The necessary procedurethrough which these principles may be mastered is thoroughly described in the sixteenth lesson.

The development of personal power is but the first step to be taken in the development of the potential power that is available through the medium of allied effort, or co-operation, which may be called group power.

It is a well known fact that all men who have amassed large fortunes have been known as able "organizers." By this is meant that they possessed the ability to enlist the co-operative efforts of other men who supplied talent and ability which they, themselves, did not possess.

The chief object of this course is so to unfold the principles of organized and co-operative or allied effort that the student will comprehend their significance and make them the basis of his philosophy.

Take, as an example, any business or profession that you choose and you will observe, by analysis, that it is limited only by lack of application of organized and co-operative effort. As an illustration, consider the legal profession.

If a law firm consists of but one type of mind it will be greatly handicapped, even though it may be made up of a dozen able men

50

of this particular type. The complicated legal system calls for a greater variety of talent than any one man could possibly provide.

It is evident, therefore, that mere organized effort is not sufficient to insure outstanding success; the organization must consist of individuals each of whom supplies some specialized talent which the other members of the organization do not possess.

A well organized law firm would include talentthat was specialized in the preparation of cases; men of vision and imagination who understood how to harmonize the law and the evidence of a case under a sound plan. Men who have such ability are not always possessed of the ability to try a case in court; therefore, men who are proficient in court procedure must be available. Carrying the analysis a step further, it will be seen that there are many different classes of cases which call for men of various types of specialized ability in both the preparation and the trial of these cases. A lawyer who had prepared himself as a specialist in corporation law might be wholly unprepared to handle a case in criminal procedure.

In forming a law partnership, the man who understood the principles of organized, co-operative effort, would surround himself with talent that was specialized in every branch of law and legal procedure in which he intended to practice. The man who had no conception of the potential power of these principles would probably select his associates by the usual "hit or miss" method, basing his selections more upon personality or acquaintanceship than consideration of the particular type of legal talent that each possessed.

The subject of organized effort has been covered in the preceding lessons of this course, but it is again brought up in connection with this lesson for the purpose of indicating the necessity of forming alliances or organizations consisting of individuals who supply all of the necessary talent that may be needed for the attainment of the object in mind.

In nearly all commercial undertakings, there is a need for at least three classes of talent; namely, buyers, salesmen and those who are familiar with finance. It will be readily seen that when these three classes of men organize and co-ordinate their efforts they avail themselves, through this form of co-operation, of power which no single individual of the group possesses.

Many a business fails because all of the men back of it are salesmen, or financial men or buyers. By nature, the most able salesmen are optimistic, enthusiastic and emotional; while able financial men, as a rule, are unemotional, deliberate and conservative. Both classes are essential to the success of a commercial enterprise; but either class will prove too much of a load for any business, without the modifying influence of the other class.

It is generally conceded that James J. Hill was the most efficient railroad builder that America ever produced; but it is equally well known that he was not a civil engineer, nor a bridge builder, nor a locomotive engineer, nor a mechanical engineer, nor a chemist, although these highly specialized classes of talent are essential in railroad building. Mr. Hill understood the principles of organized effort and co-operation; therefore, he surrounded himself with men who possessed all this necessary ability which he lacked.

The modern department store is a splendid example of organized, co-operative effort.

Each merchandising department is under the management of one who understands the purchasing and marketing of the goods carried in that department.

Back of all these department managers is a general staff consisting of specialists in buying, selling, financing, and the management of units, or groups, of people. This form of organized effort places back of each department both buying andselling power such as that department could not afford if it were separated from the group and had to be operated under its own overhead, in a separate location.

The United States of America is one of the richest and most powerful nations of the world. Upon analysis, it will be seen that this enormous power has grown out of the co-operative efforts of the states of the Union.

It was for the purpose of saving this power that the immortal Lincoln made up his mind to erase the Mason and Dixon line. The saving of the Union was of far greater concern to him than was the freedom of the slaves of the South. Had this not been so, the present status of the United States as a power among the nations of the world would be far different from what it is.

It was this same principle of co-operative effort that Woodrow Wilson had in mind when he created his plan for a League of

Nations. He foresaw the need of such a plan as a medium for preventing war between nations; just as Lincoln foresaw it as a medium for harmonizing the efforts of the people of the United States, thereby preserving the Union.

Thus it is seen that the principle of organized, co-operative effort through the aid of which the individual may develop personal power, is the selfsame principle that must be employed in developing group power.

Andrew Carnegie easily dominated the steel business during his active connection with that industry, for the reason that he took advantage of the principle of organized, co-operative effort by surrounding himself with highly specialized financial men, chemists, sales managers, buyers of rawmaterials, transportation experts and others whose services were essential to that industry. He organized this group of "co-operators" into what he called a "Master Mind."

Any great university affords an excellent example of the necessity of organized, co-operative effort. The professorate is made up of men and women of highly specialized, though vastly different, ability. One department is presided over by experts in literature; another department by expert mathematicians; another department by experts in chemistry; another department by experts in economic philosophy; another department by experts in medicine; another, by experts in law, etc. The university, as a whole, is the equivalent of a group of colleges each of which is directed by experts in its own line, whose efficiency is greatly increased through allied or co-operative effort that is directed by a single head.

Analyze power, no matter where, or in what form, it may be found, and you will find organization and co-operation as the chief factors back of it. You will find these two principles in evidence in the lowest form of vegetation no less than in the highest form of animal, which is man.

. . . . . . . .

Off the coast of Norway is the most famous and irresistible maelstrom in the world. This great whirlpool of ceaseless motion has never been known to give UP any victim who was caught in its circling embrace of foaming water.

No less sure of destruction are those unfortunate souls who are caught in the great maelstrom of life toward which all who do not understand the principleof organized, co-operative effort are traveling. We are living in a world in which the law of the survival of the fittest is everywhere in evidence. Those who are "fit" are those who have power, and power is organized effort.

Unfortunate is the person who either through ignorance, or because of egotism, imagines that he can sail this sea of life in the frail bark of independence. Such a person will discover that there are maelstroms more dangerous than any mere whirlpool of unfriendly waters. All natural laws and all of Nature's plans are based upon harmonious, co-operative effort, as all who have attained high places in the world have discovered.

Wherever people are engaged in unfriendly combat, no matter what may be its nature, or its cause, one may observe the nearness of one of these maelstroms that awaits the combatants.

Success in life cannot be attained except through peaceful, harmonious, co-operative effort. Nor can success be attained single-handed or independently. Even though a man live as a hermit in the wilderness, far from all signs of civilization, he is, nevertheless, dependent upon forces outside of himself for an existence. The more he becomes a part of civilization the more dependent upon co-operative effort he becomes.

Whether a man earns his living by days' work or from the interest on the fortune he has amassed, bee will earn it with less opposition through friendly co- operation with others. Moreover, the man whose philosophy is based upon co-operation instead of competition will not only acquire the necessities and the luxuries of life with less effort, but he will enjoyan extra reward in happiness such as others will never feel.

Fortunes that are acquired through co-operative effort inflict no scars upon the hearts of their owners, which is more than can be said of fortunes that are acquired through conflict and competitive methods that border on extortion.

The accumulation of material wealth, whether the object is that of bare existence or luxury, consumes most of the time that we put into this earthly struggle. If we cannot change this materialistic tendency of human nature, we can, at least, change the method of pursuing it by adopting co-operation as the basis of the pursuit.

Co-operation offers the two-fold reward of providing one with both the necessities and the luxuries of life and the peace of mind which the covetous never know. The avaricious and covetous person may amass a great fortune in material wealth; there is no denying this fact; but he will have sold his soul for a mess of pottage in the bargain.

Let us keep in mind the fact that all success is based upon power, and power grows out of knowledge, that has been organized and expressed in terms of ACTION.

The world pays for but one kind of knowledge, and that is the kind which is expressed in terms of constructive service. In addressing the graduating class of a business college one of the best known bankers in America said:

"You ought to feel proud of your diplomas, because they are evidence that you have been preparing yourselves for action in the great field of business.

"One of the advantages of a business college training is that it prepares you for action! Not to belittle other methods of education, but to exalt the modern business college method, I am reminded to say that there are some colleges in which the majority of the students are preparing for practically everything else except action.

"You came to this business college with but one object in view, and that object is to learn to render service and earn a living. The latest style of clothing has been of little interest to you because you have been preparing yourself for work in which clothes of the latest style will play no important part. You did not come here to learn how to pour tea at an afternoon party nor to become masters at affecting friendliness while inwardly feeling envy for those who wear finer gowns and drive costly motor cars - you came here to learn how to work!"

In the graduating class before which this man spoke were thirteen boys, all of whom were so poor that they had barely enough money with which to pay their way. Some of them were paying their own way by working before and after school hours.

That was twenty-five years ago. Last summer, I met the president of the business college which these boys attended and he gave me the history of each one of them, from the time that they graduated until the time when I talked to him. One of them is the president of one of the big wholesale drug companies, and a wealthy man; one is a successful lawyer; two own large business colleges of their own; one is a professor in the department of economics in one of the largest universities in America; one is the president ofone of the large automobile manufacturing companies; two are presidents of banks, and wealthy men; one is the owner of a large department store; one is the vice-president of one of the great railway systems of the country; one is a well established Certified Public Accountant; one is dead; and the thirteenth is compiling this Reading Course on the Law of Success.

Eleven successes out of a class of thirteen boys is not a bad record, thanks to the spirit of action developed by that business college training.

It is not the schooling you have had that counts; it is the extent to which you express that which you learned from your schooling through well organized and intelligently directed action.

By no means would I belittle higher education, but I would offer hope and encouragement to those who have had no such education, provided they express that which they know, be it ever so little, in intensive action, along constructive lines.

One of the greatest Presidents who ever occupied the White House had but little schooling, but he did such a good job of expressing what knowledge he acquired by that little schooling, through properly directed action, that his name has been inseparably woven into the history of the United States.

Every city, town and hamlet has its population of those well known characters called "ne'er-do-wells," and if you will analyze these unfortunate people, you will observe that one of their outstanding features is procrastination.

Lack of action has caused them to slip backward until they got into a "rut," where they will remainunless, through accident, they are forced out into the open road of struggle where unusual action will become necessary.

Don't let yourself get into such a condition.

Every office, and every shop, and every bank, and every store, and every other place of employment has its outstanding victims of procrastination who are doing the goose-step down the dusty road of failure because they have not developed the habit of expressing themselves in action.

You can pick out these unfortunates all about you if you will begin to analyze those with whom you come in contact each day. If you will talk to them you will observe that they have built up a false philosophy somewhat of this nature:

"I am doing all I am paid to do, and I am getting by."

Yes, they are "getting by" - but that is all they are getting.

Some years ago, at a time when labor was scarce and wages unusually high, I observed scores of able-bodied men lying about in the parks of Chicago, doing nothing. I became curious to know what sort of an alibi they would offer for their conduct, so I went out one afternoon and interviewed seven of them.

With the aid of a generous supply of cigars and cigarettes and a little loose change I bought myself into the confidence of those whom I interviewed and thereby gained a rather intimate view of their philosophy. All gave exactly the same reason for being there, without employment. They said: "The world will not give me a chance!!!"

The exclamation points are my own.

Think of it - the world would not "give them a chance."

Of course the world wouldn't give them a chance.

It never gives anyone a chance. A man who wants a chance may create it through action, but if he waits for someone to hand it to him on a silver platter he will meet with disappointment.

I fear that this excuse that the world does not give a man a chance is quite prevalent, and I strongly suspect that it is one of the commonest causes of poverty and failure.

The seventh man that I interviewed on that well-spent afternoon was an unusually fine looking specimen, physically. He was lying on the ground asleep, with a newspaper over his face. When I lifted the paper from his face, he reached up, took it out of my hands, put it back over his face and went right on sleeping.

Then I used a little strategy by removing the paper from his face and placing it behind me, where he could not get it. He then sat up on the ground and I interviewed him. That fellow was a graduate from two of the great universities of the east, with a master's degree from one, and a Ph.D. from the other.

His story was pathetic.

He had held job after job, but always his employer or his fellow employee "had it in for him." He hadn't been able to make them see the value of his college training. They wouldn't "give him a chance."

Here was a man who might have been at the head of some great business, or the outstanding figure in one of the professions had he not built his house upon the sands of procrastination and held to the false be-lief that the world should pay him for what he knew!

Luckily, most college graduates do not build upon such flimsy foundations, because no college on earth can crown with success the man who tries to collect for that which he knows instead of that which he can do with what he knows.

The man to whom I have referred was from one of the best known families of Virginia. He traced his ancestry back to the landing of the Mayflower. He threw back his shoulders, pounded himself on the breast with his fist and said: "Just think of it, sir! I am a son of one of the first families of old Virginia!"

My observations lead me to believe that being the son of a "first family" is not always fortunate for either the son or the family. Too often these sons of "first families" try to slide home from third base on their family names. This may be only a peculiar notion of mine, but I have observed that the men and women who are doing the world's work have but little time, and less inclination, to brag about their ancestry.

Not long ago I took a trip back to southwest Virginia, where I was born. It was the first time I had been there in over twenty years. It was a sad sight to compare the sons of some of those who were known as "first families" twenty years ago, with the sons of those who were but plain men who made it their business to express themselves in action of the most intensive nature.

The comparison reflected no credit upon the "first family" boys! It is with no feeling of exaltation that I express my gratitude for not having been brought into the world by parents who belonged to the "first family" class. That, of course, was not a matter of choice with me, and if it had been perhaps I, too, would have selected parents of the "first family" type.

Not long ago I was invited to deliver an address in Boston, Mass. After my work was finished, a reception committee volunteered to show me the sights of the city, including a trip to Cambridge, where we visited Harvard University. While there, I observed many sons of "first families" - some of whom were equipped with Packards. Twenty years ago I would have felt proud to be a student at Harvard, with a Packard car, but the illuminating effect of my more mature years has led me to the conclusion that had I had the privilege of going to Harvard I might have done just as well without the aid of a Packard.

I noticed some Harvard boys who had no Packards. They were working as waiters in a restaurant where I ate, and as far as I could see they were missing nothing of value because they owned no Packards; nor did they seem to be suffering by comparison with those who could boast of the ownership of parents of the "first family" type.

All of which is no reflection upon Harvard University - one of the great universities of the world - nor upon the "first families" who send boys to Harvard. To the contrary, it is intended as a bit of encouragement to those unfortunates who, like myself, have but little and know but little, but express what little they know in terms of constructive, useful action.

The psychology of inaction is one of the chief reasons why some towns and cities are dying with the dry-rot!

Take the city of X, for example. You'll recognize the city by its description, if you are familiar withthis part of the country. Sunday blue-laws have closed up all the restaurants on Sunday. Railroad trains must slow down to twelve miles an hour while passing through the city. "Keep off the grass" signs are prominently displayed in the parks. Unfavorable city ordinances of one sort or another have driven the best industries to other cities. On every hand one may see evidence of restraint. The people of the streets show signs of restraint in their faces, and in their manner, and in their walk.

The mass psychology of the city is negative.

The moment one gets off the train at the depot, this negative atmosphere becomes depressingly obvious and makes one want to take the next train out again. The place reminds one of a grave-yard and the people resemble walking ghosts.

They register no signs of action!

The bank statements of the banking institutions reflect this negative, inactive state of mind. The stores reflect it in their show windows and in the faces of their salespeople. I went into one of the stores to buy a pair of hose. A young woman with bobbed hair who would have been a "flapper" if she hadn't been too lazy, threw out a box of hose on the counter. When I picked up the box, looked the hose over and registered a look of disapproval on my face, she languidly yawned:

"They're the best you can get in this dump!"

"Dump!" She must have been a mind reader, for "dump" was the word that was in my mind before she spoke. The store reminded me of a rubbish dump; the city reminded me of the same. I felt the stuff getting into my own blood. The negative psychology of thepeople was actually reaching out and gathering me in.

Maine is not the only state that is afflicted with a city such as the one I have described. I could name others, but I might wish to go into politics some day; therefore, I will leave it to you to do your own analyzing and comparing of cities that are alive with action and those that are slowly dying with the dry-rot of inaction.

I know of some business concerns that are in this same state of inaction, but I will omit their names. You probably know some, too.

Many years ago Frank A. Vanderlip, who is one of the best known and most capable bankers in America, went to work for the National City Bank, of New York City.

His salary was above the average from the start, for the reason that he was capable and had a record of successful achievement that made him a valuable man.

He was assigned to a private office that was equipped with a fine mahogany desk and an easy chair. On the top of the desk was an electric push button that led to a secretary's desk outside.

The first day went by without any work coming to his desk. The second, and third, and fourth days went by without any work. No one came in or said anything to him.

By the end of the week he began to feel uneasy. (Men of action always feel uneasy when there is no work in sight.)

The following week Mr. Vanderlip went into the president's office and said, "Look here, you are payingme a big salary and giving me nothing to do and it is grating on my nerves!"

The president looked up with a lively twinkle in his keen eyes.

"Now I have been thinking," Mr. Vanderlip continued, "while sitting in there with nothing to do, of a plan for increasing the business of this bank."

The president assured him that both "thinking" and "plans" were valuable, and asked him to continue with his interview.

"I have thought of a plan," Mr. Vanderlip went on, "that will give the bank the benefit of my experience in the bond business. I propose to create a bond department for this bank and advertise it as a feature of our business."

"What! this bank advertise?" queried the president. "Why, we have never advertised since we began business. We have managed to get along without it."

"Well, this is where you are going to begin advertising," said Mr. Vanderlip, "and the first thing you are going to advertise is this new bond department that I have planned."

Mr. Vanderlip won! Men of action usually win - that is one of their distinctive features. The National City Bank also won, because that interview was the beginning of one of the most progressive and profitable advertising campaigns ever carried on by any bank, with the result that the National City Bank became one of the most powerful financial institutions of America.

There were other results, also, that are worth naming. Among them the result that Mr. Vanderlip grew with the bank, as men of action usually grow inwhatever they help to build, until finally he became the president of that great banking house.

In the lesson on Imagination you learned how to recombine old ideas into new plans, but no matter how practical your plans may be they will be useless if they are not expressed in action. To dream dreams and see visions of the person you would like to be or the station in life you would like to obtain are admirable provided you transform your dreams and visions into reality through intensive action.

There are men who dream, but do nothing more. There are others who take the visions of the dreamers and translate them into stone, and marble, and music, and good books, and railroads, and steamships. There are still others who both dream and transform these dreams into reality. They are the dreamer-doer types.

There is a psychological as well as an economic reason why you should form the habit of intensive action. Your body is made up of billions of tiny cells that are highly sensitive and amenable to the influence of your mind. If your mind is of the lethargic, inactive type, the cells of your body become lazy and inactive also. Just as the stagnant water of an inactive pond becomes impure and unhealthful, so will the cells of an inactive body become diseased.

Laziness is nothing but the influence of an inactive mind on the cells of the body. If you doubt this, the next time you feel lazy take a Turkish bath and have yourself well rubbed down, thereby stimulating the cells of your body by artificial means, and see how quickly your laziness disappears. Or, a better way than this, turn your mind toward some game of which you are fond and notice how quickly the cells of your body will respond to your enthusiasm and your lazy feeling will disappear.

The cells of the body respond to the state of mind in exactly the same manner that the people of a city respond to the mass psychology that dominates the city. If a group of leaders engage in sufficient action to give a city the reputation of being a "live-wire" city this action influences all who live there. The same principle applies to the relationship between the mind and the body. An active, dynamic mind keeps the cells of which the physical portions of the body consist, in a constant state of activity.

The artificial conditions under which most inhabitants of our cities live have led to a physical condition known as auto-intoxication, which means self-poisoning through the inactive state of the intestines. Most headaches may be cured in an hour's time by simply cleansing the lower intestines with an enema.

Eight glasses of water a day and a reasonable amount of physical action popularly known as "exercise" will take the place of the enema. Try it for a week and then you will not have to be urged to keep it up, for you will feel like a new person, unless the nature of your work is such that you get plenty of physical exercise and drink plenty of water in the regular course of your duties.

On two pages of this book enough sound advice could be recorded to keep the average person healthy and ready for action during sixteen of the twenty-four hours of the day, but the advice would be so simple that most people would not follow it.

The amount of work that I perform every day and still keep in good physical condition is a source ofwonderment and mystery to those who know me intimately, yet there is no mystery to it, and the system I follow does not cost anything.

Here it is, for your use if you want it:

First: I drink a cup of hot water when I first get up in the morning, before I have breakfast.

Second: My breakfast consists of rolls made of whole wheat and bran, breakfast cereal, fruit, soft-boiled eggs once in a while, and coffee. For luncheon I eat vegetables (most any kind), whole wheat bread and a glass of buttermilk. Supper, a well cooked steak once or twice a week, vegetables, especially lettuce, and coffee.

Third: I walk an average of ten miles a day: five miles into the country and five miles back, using this period for meditation and thought. Perhaps the thinking is as valuable, as a health builder, as the walk.

Fourth: I lie across a straight bottom chair, flat on my back, with most of my weight resting on the small of my back, with my head and arms relaxed completely, until they almost touch the floor. This gives the nervous energy of my body an opportunity to balance properly and distribute itself, and ten minutes in this position will completely relieve all signs of fatigue, no matter how tired I may be.

Fifth: I take an enema at least once every ten days, and more often if I feel the need of it, using water that is a little below blood temperature, with a tablespoonful of salt in it, chest and knee position.

Sixth: I take a hot shower bath, followed immediately by a cold shower, every day, usually in the morning when I first get up.

These simple things I do for myself. Mother Nature attends to everything else necessary for my health.

I cannot lay too much stress upon the importance of keeping the intestines clean, for it is a well known fact that the city dwellers of today are literally poisoning themselves to death by neglecting to cleanse their intestines with water. You should not wait until you are constipated to take an enema. When you get to the stage of constipation you are practically ill and immediate relief is absolutely essential, but if you will give yourself the proper attention regularly, just as you attend to keeping the outside of your body clean, you will never be bothered with the many troubles which constipation brings.

For more than fifteen years no single week ever passed without my having a headache. Usually I administered a dose of aspirin and got temporary relief. I was suffering with auto-intoxication and did not know it, for the reason that I was not constipated.

When I found out what my trouble was I did two things, both of which I recommend to you; namely, I quit using aspirin and I cut down my daily consumption of food nearly one half.

Just a word about aspirin - a word which those who profit by its sale will not like - it affords no permanent cure of headache. All it does might be compared to a lineman that cuts the telegraph wire while the operator is using that wire in a call for aid from the fire department to save the burning building in which he is located. Aspirin cuts or "deadens" the line of nerve communication that runs from the stomach or the intestinal region, where auto-intoxication is pouring poison into the blood, to thebrain, where the effect of that poison is registering its call in the form of intense pain.

Cutting the telegraph line over which a call for the fire department is being sent does not put out the fire; nor does it remove the cause to deaden, with the aid of a dose of aspirin, the nerve line over which a headache is registering a call for help.

You cannot be a person of action if you permit yourself to go without proper physical attention until auto-intoxication takes your brain and kneads it into an inoperative mass that resembles a ball of putty. Neither can you be a person of action if you eat the usual devitalized concoction called "white bread" (which has had all the real food value removed from it) and twice as much meat as your system can digest and properly dispose of.

You cannot be a person of action if you run to the pill bottle every time you have, or imagine you have, an ache or a pain, or swallow an aspirin tablet every time your intestines call on your brain for a douche bag of water and a spoonful of salt for cleansing purposes.

You cannot be a person of action if you overeat and under-exercise.

You cannot be a person of action if you read the patent medicine booklets and begin to imagine yourself ailing with the symptoms described by the clever advertisement writer who has reached your pocket book through the power of suggestion.

I have not touched a drug for more than five years, and I have not been either sick or ailing during that time, in spite of the fact that I perform more work each day than most men of my profession. I haveenthusiasm, endurance and action because I eat the sort of simple food that contains the body-building elements that I require, and look after the eliminative processes as carefully as I bathe my body.

If these simple and frank admissions appeal to you as being based upon common sense, take them and put them to the test, and if they serve you as well as they are serving me, both of us will have profited by the courage I had to summon to list them as a part of this lesson.

Usually, when anyone except a physician offers suggestions on the care of the body, he is immediately catalogued as a "long-haired crank," and I will admit that the analysis is often correct. In this instance, I make no stronger recommendations than this:

That you try an enema the next time you have a headache, and if any of the other suggestions appeal to you give them a trial until you are satisfied that they are either sound or unsound.

Before leaving the subject, perhaps I should explain that water which is barely luke-warm should be used for the enema for the reason that this causes the muscles of the intestines to contract, which, in turn, forces the poisonous matter out of the pores of the mucous linings. This exercises those muscles and eventually, it will so develop them that they will do their work in the natural way, without the aid of the enema. A warm water enema is very detrimental for the reason that it relaxes the muscles of the intestines, which, in time, causes them to cease functioning altogether, producing what is ordinarily referred to as the "enema habit."

With due apologies to my friends, the physicians and osteopaths and chiropractors and other health builders, I will now invite you back to that part of the subject of this lesson over which there can be no conflict of opinion as to the soundness of my counsel.

. . . . . . . .

There is another enemy which you must conquer before you can become a person of action, and that is the worry habit.

Worry, and envy, and jealousy, and hatred, and doubt, and fear are all states of mind which are fatal to action.

Any of these states of mind will interfere with, and in some instances destroy altogether, the digestive process through which the food is assimilated and prepared for distribution through the body. This interference is purely physical, but the damage does not stop here, because these negative states of mind destroy the most essential factor in the achievement of success; namely, desire to achieve.

In the second lesson of this course you learned that your definite chief aim in life should be supported by a burning desire for its realization. You can have no burning desire for achievement when you are in a negative state of mind, no matter what the cause of that state of mind may be.

To keep myself in a positive frame of mind I have discovered a very effective "gloom-chaser." That may not be a very dignified way of expressing my meaning, but since the subject of this lesson

65

is action and not dignity I will make it serve. The "gloom-chaser" to which I refer is a hearty laugh. When I feel "out of sorts" or inclined to argue with somebody oversomething that is not worthy of discussion, I know that I need my "gloom-chaser," and I proceed to get away where I will disturb no one and have a good hearty laugh. If I can find nothing really funny about which to laugh I simply have a forced laugh. The effect is the same in both cases.

Five minutes of this sort of mental and physical exercise - for it is both - will stimulate action that is free from negative tendencies.

Do not take my word for this - try it!

Not long ago I heard a phonograph record entitled, as I recall it, The Laughing Fool, which should be available to all whose dignity forbids them to indulge in a hearty laugh for their health's sake. This record was all that its name implies. It was made by a man and a woman; the man was trying to play a cornet and the woman was laughing at him. She laughed so effectively that she finally made the man laugh, and the suggestion was so pronounced that all who heard it usually joined in and had a good laugh, whether they felt like it or not.

"As a man thinketh in his heart, so is he."

You cannot think fear and act courageously. You cannot think hatred and act in a kindly manner toward those with whom you associate. The dominating thoughts of your mind - meaning by this, the strongest and deepest and most frequent of your thoughts - influence the physical action of your body.

Every thought put into action by your brain reaches and influences every cell in your body. When you think fear your mind telegraphs this thought down to the cells that form the muscles of your legs and tells those muscles to get into action and carry youaway as rapidly as they can. A man who is afraid runs away because his legs carry him, and they carry him because the fear thought in his mind instructed them to do so, even though the instructions were given unconsciously.

In the first lesson of this course you learned how thought travels from one mind to another, through the principle of telepathy. In this lesson you should go a step further and learn that your thoughts not only register themselves in the minds of other people, through the principle of telepathy, but, what is a million times more important to you to understand, they register themselves on the cells of your own body and affect those cells in a manner that harmonizes with the nature of the thoughts.

To understand this principle is to understand the soundness of the statement: "As a man thinketh in his heart, so is he."

Action, in the sense that the term is used in this lesson, is of two forms. One is physical and the other is mental. You can be very active with your mind while your body is entirely inactive, except as to the involuntary action of the vital organs. Or you can be very active with both body and mind.

In speaking of men of action, either or both of two types may be referred to. One is the care-taker type and the other is the promoter or salesman type. Both of these types are essential in modern business, industry and finance. One is known as a "dynamo" while the other is often referred to as a "balance wheel." Once in a great while you will find a man who is both a dynamo and a balance wheel, but such wellbalanced personalities are rare. Most successful business organizations that assume great size are made up of both of these types.

The "balance wheel" who does nothing but compile facts and figures and statistics is just as much a man of action as the man who goes upon the platform and sells an idea to a thousand people by the sheer power of his active personality. To determine whether a man is a man of action or not it is necessary to analyze both his mental and his physical habits.

In the first part of this lesson I said that "the world pays you for what you do and not for what you know." That statement might easily be misconstrued. What the world really pays you for is what you do or what you can get others to do.

A man who can induce others to co-operate and do effective team-work, or inspire others so that they become more active, is no less a man of action than the man who renders effective service in a more direct manner.

In the field of industry and business there are men who have the ability so to inspire and direct the efforts of others that all under their direction accomplish more than they could without this directing influence. It is a well known fact that Carnegie so ably directed the efforts of those who constituted his personal staff that he made many wealthy men of those who would never have become wealthy without the directing genius of his brain. The same may be said of practically all great leaders in the field of industry and business - the gain is not all on the side of the leaders. Those under their direction often profit most by their leadership.

It is a common practice for a certain type of man to berate his employers because of their opposite stations in a financial sense. It is usually true that such men would be infinitely worse off without these employers than they are with them.

In the first lesson of this course the value of allied effort was particularly emphasized for the reason that some men have the vision to plan while others have the ability to carry plans into action although they do not possess the imagination or the vision to create the plans they execute.

It was his understanding of this principle of allied effort that enabled Andrew Carnegie to surround himself with a group of men that was made up of those who could plan and those who could execute. Carnegie bad in his group of assistants some of the most efficient salesmen in the world, but if his entire staff had been made up of men who could do nothing but sell he could never have accumulated the fortune that he did. If his entire staff had been made up of salesmen only he would have had action in abundance, but action, in the sense that it is used in this lesson, must be intelligently guided.

One of the best known law firms in America is made up of two lawyers, one of whom never appears in court. He prepares the firm's cases for trial and the other member of the firm goes to court and tries them. Both are men of intense action, but they express it in different ways.

There can be as much action in preparation, in most undertakings, as in execution.

In finding your own place in the world, you should analyze yourself and find out whether you are a "dynamo" or a "balance wheel," and select a definite chief aim for yourself that harmonizes with your native ability. If you are in business with others, you should analyze them as well as yourself, and endeavor to see that each person takes the part for which his temperament and native ability best fit him.

Stating it another way, people may be classified under two headings: one is the promoter and the other is the care-taker. The promoter type makes an able salesman and organizer. The care-

68

taker type makes an excellent conserver of assets after they have been accumulated.

Place the care-taker type in charge of a set of books and he is happy, but place him on the outside selling and he is unhappy and will be a failure at his job. Place the promoter in charge of a set of books and he will be miserable. His nature demands more intense action. Action of the passive type will not satisfy his ambitions, and if he is kept at work which does not give him the action his nature demands be will be a failure. It very frequently turns out that men who embezzle funds in their charge are of the promoter type and they would not have yielded to temptation had their efforts been confined to the work for which they are best fitted.

Give a man the sort of work that harmonizes with his nature and the best there is in him will exert itself. One of the outstanding tragedies of the world is the fact that most people never engage in the work for which they are best fitted by nature.

Too often the mistake is made, in the selection of a life-work, of engaging in the work which seems to be the most profitable from a monetary viewpoint,without consideration of native ability. If money alone brought success this procedure would be all right, but success in its highest and noblest form calls for peace of mind and enjoyment and happiness which come only to the man who has found the work that he likes best.

The main purpose of this course is to help you analyze yourself and determine what your native ability best fits you to do. You should make this analysis by carefully studying the chart that accompanies the Introductory Lesson before you select your definite chief aim.

We come, now, to the discussion of the principle through which action may be developed. To understand how to become active requires understanding of how not to procrastinate.

These suggestions will give you the necessary instructions:

First: Form the habit of doing each day the most distasteful tasks first. This procedure will be difficult at first, but after you have formed the habit you will take pride in pitching into the hardest and most undesirable part of your work first.

Second: Place this sign in front of you where you can see it in your daily work, and put a copy in your bedroom, where it will greet you as you retire and when you arise: "Do not tell them what you can do; show them!"

Third: Repeat the following words, aloud, twelve times each night just before you go to sleep: "Tomorrow I will do everything that should be done, when it should be done, and as it should be done. I will perform the most difficult tasks first because thiswill destroy the habit of procrastination and develop the habit of action in its place."

Fourth: Carry out these instructions with faith in their soundness and with belief that they will develop action, in body and in mind, sufficient to enable you to realize your definitc chief aim.

The outstanding feature of this course is the simplicity of the style in which it is written. All great fundamental truths are simple, in final analysis, and whether one is delivering an address or writing a course of instruction, the purpose should be to convey impressions and statements of fact in the clearest and most concise manner possible.

Before closing this lesson, permit me to go back to what was said about the value of a hearty laugh as a healthful stimulant to action, and add the statement that singing produces the same effect, and in some instances is far preferable to laughing.

Billy Sunday is one of the most dynamic and active preachers in the world, yet it has been said that his sermons would lose much of their effectiveness if it were not for the psychological effect of his song services.

It is a well known fact that the German army was a winning army at the beginning, and long after the beginning of the world war; and it has been said that much of this was due to the fact that the German army was a singing army. Then came the khaki-clad doughboys from America, and they, too, were singers. Back of their singing was an enduring faith in the cause for which they were fighting. Soon the Germans began to quit singing, and as they did so the tide of war began to turn against them.

During the war I helped devise ways and means of speeding production in industrial plants that were engaged in manufacturing war supplies. By actual test, in a plant employing 3,000 men and women, the production was increased forty-five per cent in less than thirty days after we had organized the workers into singing groups and installed orchestras and bands that played at ten-minute intervals such stirring songs as "Over There," and "Dixie;" and "There'll Be a Hot Time in the Old Town

Tonight." The workers caught the rhythm of the music and speeded up their work accordingly.

Properly selected music would stimulate any class of workers to greater action, a fact which does not seem to be understood by all who direct the efforts of large numbers of people.

In all my travels I have found but one business firm whose managers made use of music as a stimulant for their workers. This was the Filene Department Store, in Boston, Mass. During the summer months this store provides an orchestra that plays the latest dance music for half an hour before opening time, inthe morning. The salespeople use the aisles of the store for dancing and by the time the doors are thrown open they are in an active state of mind and body that carries them through the entire day.

Incidentally, I have never seen more courteous or efficient salespeople than those employed by the Filene store. One of the department managers told me that every person in his department performed more service and with less real effort, as a result of the morning music program.

A singing army is a winning army, whether on the field of battle, in warfare, or behind the counters in a department store. There is a book entitled Singing Through Life With God by George Wharton James, which I recommend to all who are interested in the psychology of song.

If I were the manager of an industrial plant in which the work was heavy and monotonous, I would install some sort of musical program that would supply every worker with music. On lower Broadway, in New York City, an ingenious Greek has discovered bow to entertain his customers and at the same time speed up the work of his helpers by the use of a phonograph. Every boy in the place keeps time with the music as he draws the cloth across the shoes, and seems to get considerable fun out of his work in doing so. To speed up the work the proprietor has but to speed up the phonograph.

. . . . . . . .

Any form of group effort, where two or more peoplee form a co-operative alliance for the purpose of accomplishing a definite purpose, becomes more powerful than mere individual effort.

A football team may win consistently and continuously, by well co-ordinated team-work, even though the members of the team may be unfriendly and out of harmony in many ways outside of their actual work on the ball ground.

A group of men composing a board of directors may disagree with one another; they may be unfriendly, and in no way in sympathy with one another, and still carry on a business which appears to be very successful.

A man and his wife may live together, accumulate a fair sized or even a great fortune, rear and educate a family, without the bond of harmony which is essential for the development of a Master Mind.

But all of these alliances might be made more powerful and effective if based upon a foundation of perfect harmony, thus permitting the development of a supplemental power known as the Master Mind.

Plain co-operative effort produces power; there can be no doubt about this; but co-operative effort that is based upon complete harmony of purpose develops super-power.

Let every member of any cooperative group set his heart upon the achievement of the same definite end, in a spirit of perfect harmony, and the way has been paved for the development of a Master Mind, providing all members of the group willingly subordinate their own personal interests for the attainment of the objective for which the group is aiming.

The United States of America has become one of the most powerful nations on earth, largely because of the highly organized co-operative effort between the states. It will be helpful to remember that theseUnited States were born as the result of one of the most powerful Master Minds ever created. The members of this Master Mind were the signers of the Declaration of Independence.

The men who signed that document either consciously or unconsciously put into operation the power known as the "Master Mind," and that power was sufficient to enable them to defeat all the soldiers who were sent into the field against them. The men who fought to make the Declaration of Independence endure did not fight for money, alone; they fought for a principle - the principle of freedom, which is the highest known motivating force.

A great leader, whether in business, finance, industry or statesmanship, is one who understands how to create a motivating objective which will be accepted with enthusiasm by every member of his group of followers.

In politics a "live issue" is everything!

By "live issue" is meant some popular objective toward the attainment of which the majority of the voters can be rallied. These "issues" generally are broadcast in the form of snappy slogans, such as "Keep Cool with Coolidge," which suggested to the minds of the voters that to keep Coolidge was the equivalent of keeping prosperity. It worked!

During Lincoln's election campaign the cry was, "Stand back of Lincoln and preserve the Union." It worked.

Woodrow Wilson's campaign managers, during his second campaign, coined the slogan, "He kept us out of war," and it worked.

The degree of power created by the co-operativeeffort of any group of people is measured, always, by the nature of the motive which the group is laboring to attain. This may be profitably home in mind by all who organize group effort for any purpose whatsoever. Find a motive around which men may be induced to rally in a highly emotionalized, enthusiastic spirit of perfect harmony and you have found the starting point for the creation of a Master Mind.

It is a well known fact that men will work harder for the attainment of an ideal than they will for mere money. In searching for a "motive" as the basis for developing co-operative group effort it will be profitable to bear this fact in mind.

At the time of the writing of this lesson there is much adverse agitation and general criticism directed against the railroads of the country. Who is back of this agitation this author does not know, but he does know that the very fact that such agitation exists could and should be made the motivating force around which the railroad officials might rally the hundreds of thousands of railroad employees who earn their living by railroading, thereby creating a power that would effectively eliminate this adverse criticism.

The railroads are the very back-bone of the country. Tie up all railroad service and the people of the larger cities would starve before food could reach them. In this fact may be found a motive around which a large majority of the public could be caused to rally in support of any plan for self-protection which the railroad officials might wish to carry out.

The power represented by all of the railroad employees and a majority of the public who patronize the railroads is sufficient to protect the railroadsagainst all manner of adverse legislation and other attempts to depreciate their properties, but the power is only potential until it is organized and placed definitely back of a specific motive.

. . . . . . . .

Man is a queer animal. Give him a sufficiently vitalized motive and the man of but average ability, under ordinary circumstances, will suddenly develop superpower.

What man can and will accomplish to please the woman of his choice (providing the woman knows how to stimulate him to action) bas ever been a source of wonderment to students of the human mind.

There are three major motivating forces to which man responds in practically all of his efforts. These are:

1. The motive of self-preservation
2. The motive of sexual contact
3. The motive of financial and social power.

Stated more briefly, the main motives which impel men to action are money, sex and self-preservation. Leaders who are seeking a motivating force out of which to secure action from a following may find it under one or more of these three classifications.

As you have observed, this lesson is very closely related to the Introductory Lesson and Lesson Two which cover the Law of the Master Mind. It is possible for groups to function co-operatively, without thereby creating a Master Mind, as, for example, where people co-operate merely out of necessity, without the spirit of harmony as the basis of their efforts. This sort of co-operation may produceconsiderable power, but nothing to compare with that which is possible when every person in an alliance subordinates his or her own individual interests and co-ordinates his or her efforts with those of all other members of the alliance, in perfect harmony.

The extent to which people may be induced to co-operate, in harmony, depends upon the motivating force which impels them to action. Perfect harmony such as is essential for creating a Master Mind can be obtained only when the motivating force of a group is sufficient to cause each member of the group completely to forget his or her own personal interests and work for the good of the group, or for the sake of attaining some idealistic, charitable or philanthropic objective.

The three major motivating forces of mankind have been here stated for the guidance of the Leader who wishes to create plans for securing cooperation from followers who will throw themselves into the carrying out of his plans in a spirit of unselfishness and perfect harmony.

Men will not rally to the support of a leader in such a spirit of harmony unless the motive that impels them to do so is one that will induce them to lay aside all thoughts of themselves.

We do well that which we love to do, and fortunate is the Leader who has the good judgment to bear this fact in mind and so lay his plans that all his followers are assigned parts that harmonize with this law.

The leader who gets all there is to be had from his followers does so because he has set up in the mind of each a sufficiently strong motive to get each to subordinate his own interests and work in a perfect spirit of harmony with all other members of the group.

Regardless of who you are, or what your definite chief aim may be, if you plan to attain the object of your chief aim through the co-operative efforts of others you must set up in the minds of those whose cooperation you seek a motive strong enough to insure their full, undivided, unselfish co-operation, for you will then be placing back of your plans the power of the Law of the Master Mind.

. . . . . . . .

You are now ready to take up Lesson Fourteen, which will teach you how to make working capital out of all mistakes, errors and failures which you have experienced, and also how to profit by the mistakes and failures of others.

The president of one of the great railway systems of the United States said, after reading the next lesson, that "this lesson carries a suggestion which, if heeded and understood, will enable any person to become a master in his chosen life-work."

For reasons which will be plain after you have read the next lesson, it is the author's favorite lesson of this course.

# YOUR STANDING ARMY

## An After-the-Lesson Visit With the Author

(These fifteen soldiers are labeled: Definite Chief Aim, Self-Confidence, Habit of Saving, Imagination, Initiative and Leadership, Enthusiasm, Self-Control, Doing More Than Paid For, Pleasing Personality, Accurate Thought, Concentration, Co-operation, Failure, Tolerance, Golden Rule)

Power comes from organized effort. You see in the above picture the forces which enter into all organized effort. Master these fifteen forces and you may have whatever you want in life. Others will be helpless to defeat your plans. Make these fifteen forces your own and you will be an accurate thinker.

IN the picture at the top of this page you see the most powerful army on earth! Observe the emphasis on the word POWERFUL.
This army is standing at attention, ready to do the bidding of any person who will command it. It is YOUR army if you will take charge of it.
This army will give you POWER sufficient tomow down all opposition with which you meet. Study the picture carefully, then take inventory of yourself and find out how many of these soldiers you need.
. . . . . . . .
If you are a normal person you long for material success.
Success and POWER are always found together. You cannot be sure of success unless you have power. You cannot have power unless you develop it through fifteen essential qualities.
Each of these fifteen qualities may be likened to the commanding officer of a regiment of soldiers. Develop these qualities in your own mind and you will have POWER.
The most important of the fifteen commanding officers in this army is DEFINITE PURPOSE.
Without the aid of a definite purpose the remainder of the army would be useless to you. Find out, as early in life as possible, what your major purpose in life shall be. Until you do this you are

76

nothing but a drifter, subject to control by every stray wind of circumstance that blows in your direction.

Millions of people go through life without knowing what it is they want.

All have a purpose, but only two out of every hundred have a DEFINITE purpose. Before you decide whether your purpose is DEFINITE or not, look up the meaning of the word in the dictionary.

NOTHING IS IMPOSSIBLE TO THE PERSON WHO KNOWS WHAT IT IS HE WANTS AND MAKES UP HIS MIND TO ACQUIRE IT!

Columbus had a DEFINITE PURPOSE and it be-came a reality. Lincoln's major DEFINITE PURPOSE was to free the black slaves of the South and he turned that purpose into reality. Roosevelt's major purpose, during his first term of office, was to build the Panama Canal. He lived to see that purpose realized. Henry Ford's DEFINITE PURPOSE was to build the best popular priced automobile on earth. That purpose, backed persistently, has made him the most powerful man on earth. Burbank's DEFINITE PURPOSE was to improve plant life. Already that purpose has made possible the raising of enough food on ten square miles of land to feed the entire world.

. . . . . . . .

Twenty years ago Edwin C. Barnes formed a DEFINITE PURPOSE in his mind. That purpose was to become the business partner of Thomas A. Edison. At the time his purpose was chosen Mr. Barnes had no qualification entitling him to a partnership with the world's greatest inventor. Despite this handicap he became the partner of the great Edison. Five years ago he retired from active business, with more money than he needs or can use, wealth that he accumulated in partnership with Edison.

NOTHING IS IMPOSSIBLE TO THE MAN WITH A DEFINITE PURPOSE!

Opportunity, capital, co-operation from other men and all other essentials for success gravitate to the man who knows what he wants!

Vitalize your mind with a DEFINITE PURPOSE and immediately your mind becomes a magnet which attracts everything that harmonizes with that purpose.

James J. Hill, the great railroad builder, was a poorly paid telegraph operator. Moreover, he had reached the age of forty and was still ticking away at the telegraph key without any outward appearances of success.

Then something of importance happened! Of importance to Hill and to the people of the United States. He formed the DEFINITE PURPOSE of building a railroad across the great waste desert of the West. Without reputation, without capital, without encouragement from others James J. Hill got the capital and built the greatest of all the railroad systems of the United States.

Woolworth was a poorly paid clerk in a general store. In his mind's eye he saw a chain of novelty stores specializing on five and ten cent sales. That chain of stores became his DEFINITE PURPOSE. He made that purpose come true, and with it more millions than he could use.

Cyrus H. K. Curtis selected, as his DEFINITE PURPOSE, the publishing of the world's greatest magazine. Starting with nothing but the name "Saturday Evening Post," and opposed by friends and advisers who said "It couldn't be done," he transformed that purpose into reality.

Martin W. Littleton is the most highly paid lawyer in the world. It is said that he will accept no retainer under $50,000.00. When he was twelve years old he had never been inside of a school boom. He went to hear a lawyer defend a murderer. That speech so impressed him that he grabbed hold of his father's hand and said, "Some day I am going to be the bestlawyer in the United States and make speeches like that man."

"Fine chance for an ignorant mountain youth to become a great lawyer," someone might say, but remember that NOTHING IS IMPOSSIBLE TO THE MAN WHO KNOWS WHAT HE WANTS AND MAKES UP HIS MIND TO GET IT.

. . . . . . . .

Study each of the fifteen soldiers shown in command of the army in the picture at the beginning of this essay.

Remember, as you look at the picture, that no one of these soldiers alone is powerful enough to insure success. Remove a single one of them and the entire army would be weakened.

The powerful man is the man who has developed, in his own mind, the entire fifteen qualities represented by the fifteen commanding officers shown in the picture. Before you can have power you must have a DEFINITE PURPOSE; you must have SELF-CONFIDENCE with which to back up that purpose; you must have INITIATIVE and LEADERSHIP with which to exercise your self-confidence; you must have IMAGINATION in creating your definite purpose and in building the plans with which to transform that purpose into reality and put your plans into action. You must mix ENTHUSIASM with your action or it will be insipid and without "kick." You must exercise SELF-CONTROL. You must form the habit of DOING MORE THAN PAID FOR. You must cultivate a PLEASING PERSONALITY. You must acquire theHABIT OF SAVING. You must become an ACCURATE THINKER, remembering, as you develop this quality, that accurate thought is based upon FACTS and not upon hearsay evidence or mere information. You must form the habit of CONCENTRATION by giving your undivided attention to but one task at a time. You must acquire the habit of CO-OPERATION and practice it in all your plans. You must profit by FAILURE, your own and that of others. You must cultivate the habit of TOLERANCE. Last, but by no means the least important, you must make the GOLDEN RULE the foundation of all you do that affects other people.

Keep this picture where you can see it each day and, one by one, call these fifteen soldiers out of the line and study them. Make sure that the counterpart of each is developed in your own mind.

· · · · · · · ·

All efficient armies are well disciplined!

The army which you are building in your own mind must, also, be disciplined. It must obey your command at every step,

When you call out of the line the thirteenth soldier, "FAILURE," remember that nothing will go as far toward developing discipline as will failure and temporary defeat. While you are comparing yourself with this soldier determine whether or not you have been profiting by your own failures and temporary defeat.

FAILURE comes to all at one time or another. Make sure, when it comes your way, that you will learn something of value from its visit. Make sure,also, that it would not visit you if there was not room for it in your make-up.

To make progress in this world you must rely solely upon the forces within your own mind for your start. After this start has been made you may turn to others for aid, but the first step must be taken without outside aid.

After you have made this "start," it will surprise you to observe how many willing people you will encounter who will volunteer to assist you.

. . . . . . . .

Success is made up of many facts and factors, chiefly of the fifteen qualities represented by these fifteen soldiers. To enjoy a well balanced and rounded out success one must appropriate as much or as little of each of these fifteen qualities as may be missing in one's own inherited ability.

When you came into this world you were endowed with certain inborn traits, the result of millions of years of evolutionary changes, through thousands of generations of ancestors.

Added to these inborn traits you acquired many other qualities, according to the nature of your environment and the teaching you received during your early childhood. You are the sum total of that which was born in you and that which you have picked up from your experiences, what you have thought and what you have been taught, since birth.

Through the law of chance one in a million people will receive, through inborn heredity and from knowledge acquired after birth, all of the fifteen qualities named in the picture above.

All who are not fortunate enough to have thus acquired the essentials for SUCCESS must develop them within themselves.

The first step in this "development" process is to realize what qualities are missing in your naturally acquired equipment. The second step is the strongly planted DESIRE to develop yourself where you are now deficient.

Prayer sometimes works, while at other times it does not work.

It always works when backed with unqualified FAITH. This is a truth which no one will deny, yet, it is a truth which no one can explain. All we know is that prayer works when we BELIEVE it will work. Prayer without FAITH is nothing but an empty collection of words.

A DEFINITE PURPOSE may be transformed into reality only when one BELIEVES it can be done. Perhaps the selfsame law that turns the prayer based upon FAITH into reality transforms, also, a DEFINITE PURPOSE that is founded upon belief into reality.

It can do no harm if you make your DEFINITE PURPOSE in life the object of your daily prayer. And, as you pray remember that prayer based upon FAITH always works.

Develop in your own mind all of the fifteen qualities, from a DEFINITE PURPOSE to the GOLDEN RULE, and you will find the application of FAITH is not difficult.

Take inventory of yourself. Find out how many of the fifteen qualities you now possess. Add to this inventory the missing qualities until you have, in yourmind, the entire fifteen. You will then be ready to measure your success in whatever terms you DESIRE.

The qualities represented by the fifteen soldiers shown in this picture are the brick and the mortar and the building material with which you must build your Temple of Success. Master these fifteen qualities and you may play a perfect symphony of success in any undertaking, just as one who has mastered the fundamentals of music may play any piece at sight.

Make these fifteen qualities your own and you will be an EDUCATED person, because you will have the power to get whatever you want in life without violating the rights of others.

"All worlds are man's, to conquer and to rule
This is the glory of his life.
But this its iron law: first must he school
Himself. Here 'gins and ends all strife."

# BN Publishing
# We have Book Recommendations for you

*Automatic Wealth: The Secrets of the Millionaire Mind--Including: Acres of Diamonds, As a Man Thinketh, I Dare you!, The Science of Getting Rich, The Way to Wealth, and Think and Grow Rich*
by Napoleon Hill, et al

*Think and Grow Rich [MP3 AUDIO] [UNABRIDGED]*
by Napoleon Hill, Jason McCoy (Narrator)

*As a Man Thinketh [UNABRIDGED]*
by James Allen, Jason McCoy (Narrator)

*Your Invisible Power: How to Attain Your Desires by Letting Your Subconscious Mind Work for You [MP3 AUDIO] [UNABRIDGED]*
by Genevieve Behrend, Jason McCoy (Narrator)

*Thought Vibration or the Law of Attraction in the Thought World [MP3 AUDIO] [UNABRIDGED]*
by William Walker Atkinson, Jason McCoy (Narrator)

**BN Publishing**
Improving People's Life
www.bnpublishing.com

Printed in the United States
66541LVS00004B/16-18

9 789562 912082